Ariaaisms

Spiritual Food for the Soul

Ariaa Jaeger

Copyright © 2013 Ariaa Jaeger

Cover design by Ariaa Jaeger/ Jeff Davis, photographer

Back cover photography by Kris Davis

Book design by Ariaa Jaeger

Edit/formatting and back cover design by Robbin Simons

All rights reserved. No part of this book may be reproduced by any means, in any form, graphic, electronic, or by mechanical means including photocopying, recording, taping, or by any information storage and retrieval systems, without the written permission of the author, except for the purposes of professional articles or critical reviews.

Autographed copies of this book may be purchased at the author's website,

www.Ariaa.com

ISBN: 978-0-9895503-8-3 (sc) ISBN: 978-0-9895503-3-8 (e)

Printed in the United States of America

First Printing: August 2013

10 9 8 7 6 5 4 3 2 1

Visit my website: www.Ariaa.com

The intent of the author is to offer information of a spiritual and practical nature to help you in your quest for a more fulfilling life. The author does not dispense medical advice and any practices implemented from reading this book are at the sole discretion of the reader and are not the responsibility of the author.

Have I told you how much I love you, how much you add to the depth and breadth of my life…..I will….

Dedicated to Michael Jaeger

Thank you for being a continued blessing to me for more than 22 years with your love, support and the sharing of your unique perspectives on life and spirituality. Without you I would not be all that I have become. You will always hold a special place in my heart and will always have my unconditional love, my deepest affection and my undying loyalty.

My deepest love and gratitude to Ruth Paulson and Jean Arena, my angels on earth, who through thick or thin have loved and supported me through every fire, every storm and every sunrise. You women are an amazing gift to my heart, soul and life and your love has given me wings.

To my beloved friends Kris and Jeff Davis who have gone beyond every limitation in friendship to love, support and encourage me, I will be eternally grateful to both of you and all the blessings you have so lovingly showered upon me. You have been there when others were not and have proven yourselves to be devoted friends and extraordinary human beings.

Table of Contents

Forward by Dr. Mia Rose	1
Introduction ~ A Message from Ariaa	5
Genesis Rising	10
A Spiritual Oddity ~ Walk-ins Welcomed	16
The Enigmatic Kaleidoscope	30
Journey to the Sacred Self	38
The Pedestal Principle	84
The Consummate Sage ~ Lessons from Divine Mind	92
Behold the Vision ~ A Walk in Wisdom	142
The Shadows Edge	176
The Rabid Seed	188
The Mountain's Echo ~ Ask, Speak, Find	211
The Wisdom of the Sages ~ Beyond the Veil	226
Ariaa's Ark ~ All Creatures Great and Small	261
Psalms from the Soul ~ Parables for Conscious Living	279
Poetic Rhythms for the Dance of Life	303
Pathways to Love ~ My Blessing to You	354
Acknowledgements	357

Ariaaisms

Spiritual Food for the Soul

Foreword

Welcome. You hold in your hands a gift of love. I personally thank the Holy Spirit, the universe, and all the angels for the whispers that encouraged Ariaa to bless the world with this remarkable treasure chest of personal experience, reflections, teachings and poetic inspiration.

Life often has a way of rocking the very foundation of our being, leaving us feeling lonely, flawed, undesirable, hopeless, powerless, and empty. This book is about the extraordinary spiritual path we all find ourselves on, and how it's possible to emerge from darkness into the sacred light of LOVE. Ariaa tells the fascinating story of her own awakening that came through a near death experience in Austria. On that miraculous day, a window opened into a whole new dimension where she experienced firsthand that there is so much more to life than what we experience through our physical senses. The spiritual journey is, in fact, far more breathtaking, awe-inspiring, and exciting than we could possibly imagine.

With the Holy Spirit as her guide, Ariaa's authentic self-awareness encourages the same transformation in others that she had experienced herself. In fact, everyone who energetically enters into her presence can't help but sense her genuineness and humor, and enjoy the heart-to-heart connections that she creates. Ariaa exudes a heightened consciousness that allows her to see others with great compassion and clarity. Her encouraging being is as gentle as flowing water as she courageously explores the mysteries of the universe, and celebrates the splendor, beauty and magnificence of the human spirit.

Ariaa teaches that we already possess the wisdom within, but to bring about a genuine transformation of consciousness and become all we could be, there must arise within us a commitment to refocus our attention on what she describes as "a higher way of thinking, a more evolved way of living and a more loving way of being." Each and every one of us has the potential to become enlightened by embracing our soul's whispers. We can't control the outside world, but we can create a sense of purpose within that brings about deep satisfaction and personal peace – regardless of what is going on around us. Connecting with the divine is the most authentic, lasting power we have in our lives.

Ariaa has such magnificence to share... the light that she beams into the world is not only unique, but also very powerful. What I admire most about Ariaa is her passion to serve humanity. This incredibly lovely, generous, and caring individual works intimately with thousands of men and women all over the world to help them step into their power, feel excited by a purpose, deal with challenges, face disappointment with grace, and live by an intuitive guiding wisdom.

Ariaa demonstrates in the most loving way possible that we need to make room for miracles. As a spiritual teacher, she is intimately connected with the flow of life that reminds us that whoever we are, whatever our souls were meant to accomplish, whatever lessons we were born to learn, now is the time to awaken. She demonstrates how her own life experiences had humbled her into purity. She truly understands what each breath of life is for.

Ariaa is one of the finest spiritual guides of our time. Her own passage from death to new life breathes truth into every word she writes. The long and winding journey she had taken only adds to the luminosity of her being. If you immerse yourself in this book, you'll find layers of insight that will lead you to a fabulous sense of awakening and joy. Within your ability to reflect on your own life is your greatest power to change it. You have a destiny to fulfill – a destiny of a life that is finally, truly lived. As you read, you'll sense Ariaa's vibration, feel her presence, and know that she believes in you.

Ariaa leaves me in awe. Her Ariaaisms provide balm for the soul and her poetic gift shines through on every page. She generously informs us while guiding us toward the deep, quiet river of wisdom that saturates each and every day of our lives.

Ariaa's message quickly cuts through barriers and speaks to our deepest essence. Her words soothe and invigorate and show how we can find our truest path to happiness. The answer to some of humanity's biggest challenges is not somewhere out there for someone else to solve – it is found within and it is up to each of us personally to be the solution. This book helps us to become an agent of change, and live a more fulfilling life while contributing to the creation of a more harmonious world.

I hope you will open your heart and expand your vision of what is possible. You too can turn chaos into calm and ruin into renewal. You are whole and complete, an essential part of all that is. When you're ready to choose the extraordinary over the ordinary, turn the page… and let the transformation begin. I wholeheartedly welcome you on this beautiful mission.

Dr. Mia Rose
Psychologist and Founder of the Soulwoman Sanctuary
Editor in Chief, Soulwoman eMagazine
Author of "Awaken to Love"

Introduction
A Message from Ariaa

"You can be a cup of love or you can be the well."

I have deliberately avoided writing another book for more than ten years rather successfully. With social media sites such as Facebook and Twitter, I was able to post my quotes and "isms" and then run! I rationalized that after writing three self-published books in the 1990's and in early 2000, I had paid my dues. After all, I thought aren't the principles that I teach, live and write, old news? Sages and ancients have penned these jewels of wisdom for thousands of years. There is no new wisdom since all the answers lie within all sentient beings and as far as I can see, it is only the personalities of the teachers and deliverers of such wisdom, which differentiates the dialogue. Blowhards, babbling gurus, rajahs, monks, preachers, evangelists, psychics and even leprechauns and things that go bump in the night, have espoused these truths for ages. I continued to thwart myself with reason after reason why it was completely absurd to write another book, and told myself it was my humility that kept me from wasting a good tree to scrawl vanity-filled pages of self-indulgent, metaphysical mumbo jumbo.

Then the angels began to whisper, as they have done over the past twenty years of doing this work. At first they were sweet, soft and encouraging, nudging me on with heavenly soliloquies; then like the thunderous shrills of wanton shrews and shrilling, shrieking bridezillas, they screamed it night after night, until I reluctantly caved in from sheer exhaustion and sleep deprivation. They reminded me, that many people do have all the answers within and frankly are very aware of them, but sadly fail to apply about 90% of what the greats like Jesus, Buddha, Yogananda, Babaji and others have taught. In a world with so much technology and information, there is a severe lack of any need to go within.

So, it is in that vein that I put fingers to keyboard and began this arduous journey to teach you what you already know, the basic elements for raising your conscious awareness and becoming the self-sufficient gods you were divinely designed to be all along, liberated from disease, fear, poverty, suffering, resentments, ego, ignorance and aloneness. Galileo said, "You cannot teach a man anything; you can only help him discover it in himself." It is my ardent hope that the wisdom I have been imbued with, flows into your heart and permeates your consciousness in such a potent way, that you are instantly transformed to the highest and greatest magnitude. My sincere desire is that in these pages, you will find something useful to nurture your body, feed your mind and evolve your soul. You are never too old to learn a new way to live and you are never too young to practice the alchemy of the greatest teachers humanity has ever known. It is my sincere mission, to see all human beings embrace a higher way of thinking, a more evolved way of living and a more loving way of being.

Light is the permeate force within all things. Love is the quantitative force within all creation. There is no definition for what we call God, it is the indefinable absolute and is left in ambiguity and divinely designed, so that all may come to their own interpretation and their own understanding.

What is God you ask yourself, can we just define…
The measure of Creator paradoxically sublime?

God is not definable for truly I can say...
God is what you'd wish it be, on any given day.

For whatsoever you conceive is what form will be taken…
To help you to assimilate and not to feel forsaken.

The gravity of earth denies the soul's true memory,
The universe is full of forms, life takes that you can't see.

God is love to the twelfth power beyond all human veils,
God, the light, pure energy, pure love is what prevails.

God is power, God is joy, God intrinsic peace,
God is knowing God is life, a gross magnetic feed.

God is spirit times tenfold so great the eye can't see.
God is overwhelming love in mass delivery.

God is not a judge to you or anyone on earth,
Love resigned itself to man when Mary came to birth.

God does not decipher, for love just seeks to be...
In the mix of all your life to guide your destiny.

God has been contorted, misconstrued by greed's right hand
God the omnipresent, God the Great I AM…

Is what you are comprised of, the breathe of God, your soul
Direct amplification of the awe-inspiring whole.

Jesus said it best when he said "Know ye not you're Gods"
Moses said it with the fire which came from staff and rod.

Abraham and Gandhi and Buddha and the rest...
Taught humankind, God is the Light and that LOVE is the nest.

The challenge is to recognize, God lives inside of all,
The test today remains the same, embrace it, heed the call.

Look inside the eyes of love, in everything you pass…
See God in the homeless and in the quaking grass.

See God in the hateful and in the loving too…
See God in this poet, for I see God in you.

You won't find God in the skies if you can't see God in each other's eye.

Genesis Rising

"Remain calm when the tide approaches and the waters will transform you."

I was flying, soaring, as if I had wings lighter than air and I was free from pain. At the speed of light, I traveled through innumerable golden fields of stars, grids, constellations, and rich, vibrant, textured colors beyond those known on earth. What was taking place back down on the mountain, I cannot truthfully convey. With my lips having turned bluish-purple and my breathing suddenly nonexistent, it was apparent that my soul was no longer in my body.

For what seemed like an eternity, I was, for all intents and purposes, in what most call, heaven. The length of time that I lie there medically should have caused severe brain damage, but the harsh temperatures and frozen ground certainly helped to preserve the body. But even if we had been in a 120 degree desert, it was obvious that angels were tending to all these supernatural events, ensuring my role on the earth.

I awoke the next day at four thirty in the morning on June 17th and I shall never forget the way I felt. It was as if I was a new woman and in many ways I was. This little girl from Texas woke up speaking in a proper British accent and in the King's English! Suffice to say Michael was more than intrigued, it was as if he had a new wife altogether. Some of the first words out of my newly formed, proper, British lady mouth, like "thee" and "thou" startled him to say the least! Then I announced, "Sir, please take me to a church in the village nearby as I left something there more than 40 years ago and I need to retrieve it." Nothing this mystical ever happens without the Holy Spirit qualifying and validating it in one way or another so you don't think you are losing your mind and those around you are assured of the same.

We drove to the village in Austria where ancient churches blend in with the overbearing stone- walled castles of days gone by. I am sure Michael's cynical mind must have been reciting something to the effect of "She has got to be kidding. Whatever she is looking for will not be there!" As we walked up the long, cobblestone path which led to the ancient massive wooden doors, a man walked directly over to me and began touching my hair. I was in a pure state of being after such an elevating experience where you don't have judgment on anything, so it didn't seem odd to me. My husband ran over to my side as if to protect me, when the man started speaking in a language which sounded Turkish. When we motioned that we did not understand, he formed a few words in English, which when put together, he was asking me what I shampooed my hair with that made it so shiny. We realized in that instant that he was seeing light, not freshly washed hair but how do you explain that to someone whose language we did not speak? Michael knew in that moment that not only had my life changed but his was about to as well.

The gilded cathedral was huge, dark, and eerily as familiar as the sound of the bells tolling in the tower. I walked in, dipped my hand into the water bowl and crossed myself like a good Catholic girl but the problem was, I was not raised Catholic! My husband exclaimed, "You can't do that, your Baptist family will have a fit!" As my previous lifetime visually bombarded my mind, I was fixated on my purpose for being there so his words were just a faint echo in the distance. I walked down the long marble aisle where popes, kings and even Mozart himself, have walked. My heart began beating faster with every step. Without a moment's hesitation, I took a right turn on a row that to this day, I have no idea which one it was. As I walked to the end of the isles where Catholic Bibles lay undisturbed, collecting dust for decades, my senses directed me to one which was energetically familiar. In a mystical moment which saw my husband's jaw drop to the floor, my black onyx rosary from my last lifetime fell into my hands. You can just imagine his reaction. "How did you know it was there??? That is impossible!!!" His reaction surprised me because after all I had just died and returned with a British accent, which I thought that was far more surreal than recovering my antique rosary! "I told you sir," I replied, "The angels stood guard over it all this time."

The next few days brought even more interesting developments which not only validated that something of Biblical proportion had occurred but it became more obvious with every unexplainable phenomenon. There were so many more revelations that we found it difficult to resume a normal life.

Once you have had such a profound experience and your eyes have been opened to knowledge of previous lifetimes, how you have served and more importantly, spiritual wisdom which you did not possess before the death, you are a very different person. By mere virtue of being on the other side, in the presence of such high pure light and the beings who dwell there, you are naturally bathed and imbedded with quantum light which to say the very least, is immediately transforming.

Learning to use your newly found spiritual gifts is as individual as composing a song. The notes on the scale are the same with every piece of music but it is in the arrangement and compilation of those notes which give it your own unique signature.

As I mentioned earlier, none of these extraordinary events ever takes place without the universe, angels and the Holy Spirit validating them. There are innumerable signs and mystical events which are typically very convincing to those around you. In my case, other than knowing where to retrieve my rosary from my last lifetime, there were many vivid displays to validate me.

Over the past twenty years, there have been many events which have not only solidified my relationship with the heavenly hierarchy but have also enhanced it. Those who are intended to believe these magical happenings are given an innate knowledge; conversely, those who are not spiritually and/or emotionally evolved, will be unaccepting of any truth, much less my own.

Much like other profound Biblical events, everything spiritual in the universe, is designed to honor an individual's free will. There is no God who is going to come down to earth to tell you what you have to believe. The choices that human beings make are completely their own and are the result of their own past and current life experiences. What separates those who live actively in holy paradigms and those who live blindly and in happenstance, are the interpersonal actuation of the living god within and the implementation of the wisdom from the Ancient of Days.

Many people have had near-death experiences and while there are similarities, those who have spoken of their personal experience, have never described exactly the same thing. Again, much of it is left up to individual perceptions, similar to those who see a car accident. Everyone sees something different based on many variables including past lives, current day beliefs, fears, and mindset. So it is with spiritual phenomenon, apparitions and visions. It is highly individualized and catered to the individuals' own capacity to comprehend and delineate the information.

What I saw and how I surrendered to this majestic event, was the equivalent of having the highest wisdom divinely encoded and imprinted in my flesh. The wisdom of the Holy Spirit was then and there, seared into my mind and soul. The symmetry was a dance of perfect fusion with Divine Mind, merged in perfect convergence with my passion and desire to serve humanity.

A Spiritual Oddity Walk-ins Welcome

"Be all you were created to be, soar to heights unseen and let no man limit your range for many have forgotten how to fly."

My eyes never fully closed when at light speed, I was suddenly staring into crystal blue eyes which seemed to pierce me all the way through and a smile that sent waves of love coursing through my veins. Within nanoseconds I knew it was Jesus because the answers came even before I had fully formulated a question in my mind. He looked exactly as you would suspect, gentle, wise and radiating love from every pour. There was a peaceful calm about and from him, which transcended my soul. Beside him was an old man with white hair. I knew him too, just as I did Jesus, for both were a part of my past, long, long ago. Beside the white-haired timeless Moses, stood Abraham and beside him was Jacob and Isaac and …BUDDHA? Raised in a Southern Baptist home, the last thing I expected to see when arriving in paradise were Buddha, Krishna, Yogananda and Babaji, all standing next to the Biblical characters of my youth. There were thousands of them, angels, sages, teachers and historical figures and they surrounded me in a beautifully comfortable, cocooning circle. They all spoke without saying a word, yet I could hear their thoughts with great audibility in perfect concert and sync with one another.

For what seemed like a thousand years, Jesus led the dream conference of a lifetime, as the Holy Spirit educated me on things I could have never conceived. Heaven is similar to earth in that it is a very busy working environment, with those who have crossed over continuing to study with the wisest of the lot. Others help the newly arrived souls to assimilate to their new environment as well as helping those on earth. One vast difference is that wisdom floods your heart and mind and the ego and lower emotions no longer exist. On that side of the veil, you are in a divine state of love with a spirit of cooperation unlike any time on earth. So when "the boys" as I like to call them, began telling me who I had been in other lifetimes, my eyes were forever opened. Then they showed me the "Lambs Book of Life" also known as the Akashic records, the records of the soul, and I actually saw the living holograms of my own experiences. Even though I had not fully embraced the concept of reincarnation while living on earth, it was highly unlikely in this divine mansion world that I was going to argue with such wise souls who delivered such powerful evidence.

I want to say that I was in disbelief but that is one of the many beautiful elements of heaven's paradisiacal realm, you doubt nothing. When enfolded in such brilliant, all-consuming light, surrounded by such profound etheric beings, you succumb, because you want to drink in every moment and all of the encoded information which floods your mind. It is the equivalent of getting a thousand year education in every subject from philosophy to psychology to astronomy to science and sociology. What you have left behind on earth never occurs to you, not your loved ones, not your pets and certainly not your daily concerns. I don't mean to imply that you don't think of those you love because you do, but from a non-emotional perspective since you are keenly aware they will be fine.

You find yourself absorbing knowledge and understanding as if it were rain drenching your flesh and soaking you all the way to the bone. Your senses tell you, "I am home." What I was shown, what I was told was complex and other worldly but the basic message encompasses what I have spent the last twenty years doing, inspiring and teaching others.

There is so much more to life, the universe, parallel universes, astronomy, astrology, quantum physics and spiritual Scientifics, than most people will ever have the privilege of enveloping. The doorways are always open but few choose to enter their vast unusual world for fear of being judged or simply from fear of becoming more perhaps. Knowledge and wisdom are two different things; most want knowledge but few want insight and wisdom. Why? Because historically those who seek the higher dimensions of spiritual study are made to look like buffoons or they wind up being categorized as spiritual nut cases or new age babbling gurus. Very few men or women ever reach the level of consciousness where they are able to implement what most think of as magic or miracles. And yet Jesus himself continually reminded everyone that everything he did, everyone else could do. Why has it taken us more than 2,000 years to embrace those concepts?

I cannot imagine living any other way than with the majesty and magic of God's infinite kingdom and the skills and gifts which develop, once you strip away the ego. When you look at what is considered normal on earth, when you watch even ten minutes of television shows which highlight bad behavior and bombard the human psyche with toxic dysfunction, you wonder what is happening to our world. The dumbing down of society began decades ago but has become more like a blood sport with many networks and cable shows competing to see who and how convincingly they can shock their audience, in order to garner the greatest revenue. The fodder of fools and the dysfunctional seems to outweigh common sense, decency and self-respect. When you view what those of the earth hunger for today, it is easy to understand and embrace the teachings which help one transcend the lower fields and soar beyond the known ones, into paradigms which beget the alchemy of mastery.

When you die, you actually feel more alive than at any other time while on the earth and the reasons are many. One, you are free from the constraints of gravity which often makes us feel very weighted and heavy. Two, you are free from physical aches and pains which many people don't realize they have. Most people do not realize how much stress they are carrying in their muscles and joints. I certainly didn't before my death experience and I also did not realize that being skinny meant I lacked a concentration of light within my human body. I have an entire different perception and respect for voluptuousness now.

The heavens are full of characters and historical figures, which you would fawn and swoon over if you were on earth but in heaven your perceptions are not ego based. You see all people as equal and you view them from a heart of love and not a place of judgment. The higher you go into the myriad of varying dimensions, the more unconditional you become in your love and perceptions.

You feel very much like you did on earth and believe you still appear the same physically with one exception; you initially appear younger because we hold in our consciousness a memory of when we felt we looked our best back on earth. There are innumerable stories of people who have dreamt about their dearly departed loved ones and the commonality is that all of them appeared younger in the dreams. The amount of time that you retain an image of yourself varies depending on how much you identified with your human self and how accepting you are of your new surroundings.

Another thing most don't consider is that there are roles in the heavens just like those you portray on earth. Some on the other side work with children who die suddenly in accidents like drowning or car wrecks and some work with the elderly to help them to assimilate once they cross over, since many times they are toxic from drugs or medication. Many of those who die do not realize they have crossed over until months, even years later depending on how they died. If they die in their sleep they may not "wake up" on the other side for months but angels are sent to help them deal with their new reality. The heavens are so alive and the dynamics so seamless, that it is easy to understand why some don't see it as a different environment.

"Life is the ultimate university; make sure you graduate with honors, both the bruises and the crowns."

One of the unexpected surprises or "gifts" of raising your vibration or gaining increased light is that you begin to feel major tectonic shifts or earthquakes, especially when they occur at critical junctures like in the ring of fire. Many of my clients, especially women have been unprepared for this cosmic joke which holy books failed to record or mention, but those who study with me for any length of time, wide up with heightened sensitivities in their symbiotic relationship with mother earth.

I found out about this unique connectivity first hand. It had been eight months since that meeting on the mount and we were back in our Encino, California home, when one morning I woke up in a great deal of discomfort. I stood up and to my dismay I was crooked with my right hip higher than the left, as if a magnet was pulling at my spine. With every passing day it got worse and by the end of the seventh day I was tilted like the leaning tower of Pisa. My right hip was contorted so badly that my foot was literally 24 inches off the floor and I had to use two canes just to walk. I was in excruciating pain and though my husband and I both did not know what to do about this strange physical anomaly, my guides reassured me that it would soon be over. I was told by the angels that there was a major earthquake right underneath the house we lived in. My natural response was to call Cal Tech and announce to non-believing Scientists, that there was an earthquake within a 5 mile radius of my home to which they snickered, scoffed and dismissed me. The researcher on the other end of the phone wanted to know where I was getting my information because, she said, "There are no fault lines in the San Fernando valley."

Of course in my naiveté I told her that I was getting my information from God which to her scientific ears translated to "I'm an advocate for sugar from Candyland and I am here to force feed jelly beans and cotton candy to all mankind!" Trying to convince a scientist of the mystical is like trying to convince a giraffe to climb a tree to get a better view. Needless to say the phone call was short-lived. I hung up frustrated but wondering what harm it would do, to at the very least do a PSA (public service announcement) and have people update their earthquake supplies.

On the night of January 16, 1994, I walked into my husband's office and announced the following; "When this earthquake is over in the morning, we are outta here!" I instinctively knew that in the wee hours of January 17, 1994 at 4:30 a.m. an earthquake would rock our house and rock it is putting it mildly! With the bay window of our bedroom folding around us, my husband picked me up because I was stiff like a divining rod with electromagnetic fields riveting and racing through my 110 pound frame. We stood holding each other in the middle of the living room as the equivalent of an atom bomb exploded all around us. Grabbing our little dog "Kibbles" and hoping our cat was somewhere safe, we were paralyzed. Then the angels literally screamed in my head, "Ariaa, the gas!" Before the shaking was even done, Michael grabbed our emergency flashlight and darted out the house to turn the gas off. Sadly 57 people just 2 miles up the street did not and died in an explosion when someone lit a cigarette.

The phone rang an hour later and a researcher from Cal Tech, speaking in a very low clandestine voice said, "We would like to talk to you more about how you knew that fault line existed and was about to erupt…..but understand it has to be kept in the strictest confidence. She then acknowledged that the Northridge earthquake epicenter was not within a 5 mile radius from my house as I had predicted but was actually 3 miles from our home. That was the beginning of my understanding that these unique and heightened spiritual sensitivities and profound insights could not be ignored.

Many times we chose the ordinary over the extraordinary because the ego does not want to be made to look like a fool or because we fear losing control over our own lives. The ego masks the innate instincts which meditation and practicing spiritual principles develops and evolves.

Over the past twenty years I have not been sick once with even a cold, but being bombarded with earthquake precursor and electromagnetic fields have rendered me bedridden on many occasions. Not all earthquakes cause a disruption to my energy or life, only those on major tectonic plates or those which occur from very deep within the earth. Large earthquakes such as the December 26, 2004 Indian Ocean earthquake which was an undersea megathrust earthquake, found me in the emergency room, thirty minutes before it occurred. For weeks I had experienced growing pain in my right shoulder and even though I have an extraordinarily high threshold for pain, this was beyond my ability to handle. With Tiger Balm and Ben

Gay, I managed the severe discomfort right up until the day of the quake. I learned that I had been "birthing" a large seismic event and that the energy leaves your body the minute the quake is over. Many times as with other spiritual processes, we make it personal when it is not. After weeks of being in agonizing pain, I was beginning to believe that I had torn my shoulder's rotator cuff. My friend, who just happens to be a medical doctor, asked me to stop by the emergency clinic so he could take a quick look and an x-ray. As I suspected the x-ray revealed that I was a very healthy girl with no tear and no shoulder issues whatsoever.

As I began the short drive home, I was keenly aware that if nothing was physically wrong with me, then it had to be an earthquake. I was still very much a student navigating the waters of this strange new world of spiritual mysteries. It was a daily experiment in learning what kind of gifts I had and to what extent. How to use them was an everyday guessing game and one which was mastered through trial and error. As I was driving home from the clinic a news bulletin announced that there had just been a 9.4 earthquake and tsunami in the Indian ocean. Thousands were believed to have been killed. We soon learned that between 250,000 to 280,000 people perished on that awful day, the total number was unable to be determined since so many were swept out to sea. The day before the earthquake on Christmas morning, I awoke to a dream about a tsunami, though too late for it to be useful information.

One of the most memorable out-of-body experiences of my life occurred on February 26, 2010, only hours before one of the strongest earthquakes on record. We had already witnessed one of the deadliest earthquakes just weeks earlier on January 12, when a 7.0 quake near Haiti killed 222,521 people. For five days I was bedridden unable to do anything but lay like broccoli. My head felt like it was literally coming off from the strong precursory fields which imploded like an atom bomb! So, the week leading up to the Chile earthquake found me once again, in bed with what my friends fondly term, "handmaidens", having to tend to me and my pets, since it was virtually impossible for me to function on any real level.

On the night before the Chile quake, I was in great physical agony and beyond my threshold to handle it from too many consecutive earthquakes, occurring so close together. I spontaneously left my body. Most out-of-body experiences occur when you are not consciously attempting to leave the body and most occur with overtures of angels guiding the experience. For those of us who work on beams of light, it is common to be dispatched by angels and Spirit to other regions, in order to help someone who has just crossed over or wherever the angels feel we can be the most useful. Needless to say, the timing of this forthcoming earthquake was in sync with something which was occurring on the other side. Not only are out-of-body experiences very real, but those who experience them, marvel that they felt as though it was just another normal encounter like being with a person on earth.

After a week of sleeping through the pain of the forthcoming quake, I left my body and was instantly free of pain. With angels guiding me, I was led to a slender, lanky man who was wearing a fedora hat. There were two men flanking him on either side. The angels asked me to teach him how to get into a deep, transitional meditation to help him to assimilate. They informed me that he was in denial like many who cross over suddenly and that he was still under the belief that he was still living back on earth.

As I approached him, he did this incredible quick twirl like a spinning top and magically adjusted his black fedora. I said, "Michael, come over here please. I want to show you how to meditate." "I can't right now Ariaa, I have to get ready for my tour." It's strange how on the other side everyone automatically knows you and the name you are currently using. I was a little taken back so I repeated myself and then added, "Don't you remember that in a lecture I gave five years ago, I said you would not live to see the age of 50?" He replied, "Then we still have time because my birthday is not until next month!" I said, "Michael, sweetheart, your birthday has come and gone, it's February 2010 now. You crossed-over 8 months ago." He turned and tenderly looked me straight in the eyes and with gentle surrender came over to me and wrapped his slender arms around me. We stood there motionless holding each other, my heart pressed up to his, the purity of his spirit absolutely pierced my soul. As with all truth, in this paradisiacal realm, I instantly knew that Michael Jackson was innocent of everything, everyone on the earth had accused him of. The only thing Michael Jackson was guilty of was being profoundly pure and innocent. For such a man who had lived years ahead of his time, it was a sad irony that inside he was still just a boy. Again, all truth is instantly known when you are on the other side so there absolutely no disputing it.

We sat on a heavenly plain and talked for what seemed like an eternity as he succumbed to his new reality with gentle ease. As I rose, ready to resume life back on earth, he stood up and as we had begun, we returned to that all-encompassing, all-consuming embrace. He seemed so fragile, yet taller now that his truth had been embraced. He said and I repeat verbatim, "I want to give you something as a token of my appreciation for your helping me." Then he reached into his pocket and pulled out a small object and placed it into my hand. "It's just a small trinket but it is my favorite thing and I want you to have it." I opened my hand and there in the palm of my hand was a tiny figurine of Tinkerbelle. He reached into his other pocket and handed me a tiny figure of Jiminy Cricket. I had no conscious memory of his fondness, some call it obsession, with Neverland, Peter Pan, or Pinocchio. While I loved Michael Jackson and his incredible body of musical works, I was not a hard core fan like many were. The remainder of what was said I shall keep tucked away in my heart but when I awoke at 5:30 a.m., all I could do was sob uncontrollably.

Through puddles of tears I made my morning cup of coffee and turned on the morning news to CNN reporting that a magnitude 8.8 earthquake had just struck Maule, Chile causing widespread damage and casualties. The quake ranks as one of the ten strongest earthquakes ever recorded and was the most powerful earthquake worldwide since the 2004 Sumatran quake that triggered the massive Indian Ocean tsunami.

The pain had lifted from my body with the seismic event as usual, so after being in bed for five days I left my home in a very melancholy mood, to head to the store. How synchronous that the first thing I saw when I walked into the store was the newly released, Michael Jackson, "This Is It" DVD, in a huge display case. I grabbed it and held it to my chest trying to recapture the overwhelmingly beautiful feeling I had just hours earlier while on the other side. I wanted to buy it so badly and yet I am a very practical girl and a pretty savvy shopper. I knew that within weeks the price would decrease significantly but my heart need this! I had been moved by Michael's pure heart and our exchange and I needed this DVD, if nothing else but for comfort. I plopped down the $20.00 dollars and could not wait to watch it. On the way home I stopped to get gasoline and played a Powerball ticket which I do routinely. To my sheer delight, I won exactly $20.00 dollars on that ticket, compliments of …well, you decide.

The Enigmatic Kaleidoscope

"There is nothing easy about the journey of a thousand emotions which leads to the sphere of serene splendor."

Reaching higher levels of wisdom and accessing the concept that you have all the power within you to every element of your life, is anything but joyful. Your emotions are tamable and as you uncover the truth of your unique composition, you release the power within, but handling that truth is another thing altogether. If you fully accomplish the goal of actuating the indwelling living god and using the totality of all you are, every single moment of every single day, then expect to feel like a leper. While you will feel blessed to have these insights and gifts, many times it will make you feel like an island unless you have a very strong sense of self.

Some of your friends and those who cannot maintain the same levels of integrity and light you now dance in will fall away. Additionally, your light will act as a conduit to raise the shadows in those you interact with every day but they won't know it's your role or your light that is causing them to come out of their skin or feel uncomfortable. They will make it personal and will make it about you, thinking that you are the problem, often pointing an accusing finger at you. During those times, it may cause you to want to throw in the preverbal spiritual towel and give up, but trust me when I tell you, it is worth it to keep going. As hard as the path to living without limitation is, it is also the most rewarding thing you will ever attain or accomplish.

You must be one of two things to succeed at living the inherent life you were intended to live. You are either a very strong person with tenacity and courage or you are absolutely stark-raving mad. Few chose to take the rocky road which enables you to be free from living in fear and free from judgment and ego. But when they do, they discover a way of life that few are brave enough to engage and only a handful are able to sustain. Therefore mastery comes in varying levels so that all souls can access one degree or greater if they choose.

The ego wants to be loved, nurtured, adored, and it hungers for affection and attention. That is the human self, the skin, the body. But the soul already is complete, it knows it is love incarnate but the body and mind often repel that knowledge. The human mind is in constant competition with Divine Mind, jockeying for control. The great paradox is that Divine Mind lives within you, so you ARE in control but it is the ego you are listening to nine times out of ten.

Divine Mind is the cosmic equivalent of all knowing, all seeing, and all understanding and is only accessible when you get out of the way. It is the total sum of all of an individual's conscious experiences, the conscious and the unconscious together as a unit or in other words, the psyche. Collective conscience is another name for Divine Mind and is where all thoughts go, past, present and future. Therefore when you reach to the farthest stretches of your inner network, you access the Collective Conscience where all answers are available to you, even those events in the past and those which are a part of the future.

As you tap into your inner universe you fall in love with truth and devotion and to "The I AM" presence within you. The separation and distance you once felt from the all-knowing presence you have called God over the years, is dissolved, as you familiarize yourself with the fabric of limitless flow and certainty. Ironically, as all things in the universe are divine, you will come to see that the veil of separation you have created and encountered, the walls of falsehoods and beliefs which have helped to create that separation were also divine, for they led you to this poignant place.

The wondrousness of unlimited human potential is but miniscule compared to the vastness of the love and wonderment which dwells in the spiritual consciousness of oneness within Divine Mind. There is so much more to you and to the universe yet most people only see a limited vision. What people don't understand, they fear and that fear is the barrier which prevents the extraordinary from occurring in their ordinary lives.

I have always marveled at how people avoid the mystical because they fear it. An example would be something that happened to me on December 3, 1995, while my husband and I were living in Sedona, Arizona. It was early afternoon and as with many mystical events, the baffling and profound event which occurred came as a complete surprise. I climbed into the middle of our large California king-size bed and my head had just come to rest on the pillow and my eyes had barely closed when suddenly I was soaring so fast that I almost opened my eyes to end the experience. But as with all things mystical and spiritual I have always been one who surrenders to even the most uncomfortable spiritual happenings. And this was the happening of a lifetime so I was not about to sever it.

I soared throughout the universe seeing stars that looked like glistening balls of fire, while others appeared like crystalline cubic zirconia. It was beyond beautiful and a peace came over me like none I had known since my death in Austria. As if I had wings, I flew beyond the stars and could see the sun coming up on the other side of the earth. The earth was so magnificent. I wondered if all human beings knew how incredible our planet is but before I could even finish the thought, I was propelled by something I could not see. I felt as though there were angels flanking me on either side though I did not see them. My sight was fixed on the expanding beauty of what was up ahead. Suddenly we came upon grid lines in the heavens that looked like a spider web and in them were numbers and mathematical codes, then I came to star formations and constellations and they were in specific shapes. I had never given much thought to astrology until that moment, when the Holy Spirit opened my eyes. I realized I was seeing the constellations of Leo and Taurus all while data was encoding and imprinting my mind. I inexplicably had a vast new knowledge of the relevance and meaning behind being born under a certain astrological sign and the magnetic and scientific effects on the human being. Before I could even digest that information I was in the middle of a fabric of colors so vibrant, I began vibrating and my soul became overwhelmed. In the midst of infinity, I began soaring at what could only be perceived as lightspeed, and within nanoseconds of time, I was in the presence of the Holy of Holies, the Ancient of Days and I was before the Father God energy of all Creation. It was a split second and in that split second, the old man Michelangelo painted in the Sistine Chapel, was in my sight and holding a huge silver caldron of water which he proceeded to pour out on me. Beyond a baptismal cleansing, it felt more like a divine drowning! As rapidly as I had been taken out into the universe, I was suddenly snapped back into my body and when I opened my eyes, me and my bedding were completely drenched! The event was real! My bed was soaked and I WAS SOAKED! Astonished that the event had translated to the three dimensional world, all I could do was simply sob. I wanted to go home. The love was so overwhelming, the power of the Holy Spirit's presence was beyond anything earthly, and I was rendered a blithering blob of tears and longing. I could not speak for the remainder of the day and frankly walked a bit like a brainless zombie, mesmerized and stupefied.

"We cling to the familiar instead of reaching for the unknown where creation begins and limitation ends."

The next day one of my more evolved girlfriends called and when I told her what had happened, her response floored me. "Weren't you afraid?" she said. I said, "Afraid? No, why would

I be?" Then she remarked, "I would have thought that I just died or that I was in trouble!" I was so surprised because in that moment, I realized she still believed in a judgmental, dictatorial God and that dying was one of her fears.

What most people don't understand is that death does not mean "non-life," it simply means, "change of form." The human body dies but the soul lives on. One of Jesus' most important messages was punctuated by his resurrection. Life goes on beyond the veil of humanity. Additionally, death is simply leaving one environment and entering into another which is far more compatible to living without limitation. The idea is to bring the dimension of heaven into a living application here on earth. To transcend the ego and aspects of the earth's environment is to live as a god upon this planet, enjoying the best of both worlds. And you can have exactly that, the best of both heaven and earth in one human body.

It sounds far easier than it really is but accomplishing it begins with basic elements like healing and taming your emotions, integrating your pain, finding that which raises your joy and your spirit and sustaining the flow. Mastery is living these principles in all areas of your life. Learning to transcend a victim mentality, learning to understand and completely comprehend that there are no victims is empowering. Everything is happening exactly as it was planned by each and every soul which was ever created. Learning to detach emotionally in a way that you free others to be whatever they want to be is liberating. In other words, don't judge them for what they have chosen and don't project your fears or concerns onto the path that they have taken.

There are so many wonderful activities which facilitate reaching new levels of consciousness. Embrace laughter, embrace activities like yoga, meditation, Tai Chi, art, visiting museums, sculpting, playing a musical instrument, stargazing, walking in a place of beauty, traveling, especially to foreign countries, floating in the ocean, mountain climbing, planting a garden of beautiful flowers or growing organic vegetables, dancing in the rain; all of these things raise the vibration and spirit of human beings. There are so many more ways to elevate the soul. Avoid anything which drags you down. Avoid idle gossip and focus on keeping your karma positive. Avoid negative people and surround yourself with honest, loving, compassionate people. Work on yourself while still engaging in activities which help others. Volunteering at an assisted living center, a soup kitchen, an abused women's shelter or at an animal shelter will keep you humble. Invoking all the higher elements of integrity and goodness begins the journey that few will ever take. You may not want to reach enlightenment but like many human beings, I am almost certain you want to be the best human being you can possibly be. Just remember to keep your balance, one foot in the heavens and one foot in the earth.

Journey to the Sacred Self

"Joy doesn't happen to you, it happens within you."

Be joyful, become as a child, full of wonder and fantasy. Allow yourself the freedom to taste, touch and sense that which raises your enthusiasm. The energy of wonder brings forth new creation and the energy of joy produces more harmony in the universe, not to mention that it increases your own vibrational capacity. At one time or another while in adulthood, we harken back to a time when life was simple. In other words, we sometimes wish we could be a child again, free of adult responsibilities and full of wonder and innocence. The inner child longs to come out of the shadows into the light in every adult. When you raise the joy within, the very essence of your purity rises, thus you are more open-minded and free from limitations. That is a perfect place to begin anew, a perfect place to reform, reprogram and redesign your life. Many perceive that enlightenment and spiritual evolution require one to attain mass amounts of knowledge and severe disciplines. Many believe they cannot get there because it is simply too hard and requires too much sacrifice but the truth is simple. In fact all truth is designed to be simple so that everyone has a chance to find and embrace it. Becoming selfless and multidimensional, becoming a vehicle and instrument for healing, prophecy, increased intuition, clairvoyance, spiritual Scientifics or any of the other wondrous gifts that spiritually evolved beings possess, begins with the simplest of foundations. It begins with the basic element of loving yourself and learning how to treat you as a divine creation.

"We are here as light gatherers that we may become light beams."

Everything in the universe is energetic and vibrational. The higher your vibrational frequency, the more light you gather. The greater your light, the more you are aligned to the divine principle of the "Christ" within all. Throughout history the word, "Christ" has been directly connected to Jesus, as it should be. However what he possessed and what he taught was that the Christ principle lies within all human beings. "*...I say unto you, He that believeth on me, the works that I do shall he do also; and greater works than these shall he do*;" John 14:12. But if you look at other sages such as Buddha, Yogananda, Krishna, Babaji and others, you will find that they all subscribed to the notion that all the power of God lies within every human being. Buddha carried "Christed" energy as did modern day men like Martin Luther King, Jr. and Gandhi. Christed energy lies within all beings but those who rise to embrace an awakened consciousness, those who implement and actuate these truth principles, couple their own light with that of those who have gone before and have mastered enlightenment. The ego is then dissolved and "me" becomes "we", your total awakened oneness with all those who history has called, saints, sages and masters. When you have reached that level or remembrance of your own "Christed" perfection, you create fusion with the Divine perfection of all enlightened beings, which makes life an effortless flow of bounty, beauty and perfection.

There are many ways to retrain your mind, discipline your thoughts and increase the Christ light within you. By a constant stream of sending love and positive thoughts out each day, by meditating, praising, blessing everyone and everything and giving thanks often for even the smallest of blessings, you increase the flow of this divine energy. Additionally, it becomes more potent, more magnified and more readily available to you. From the moment I begin to awaken from a long nights slumber, I begin to praise. Even before my eyes are opened, my mind gives way to gratitude for another day of life, for the morning sun as it streams through my bedroom window while the song of the birds intoxicates my spirit. I hear the wind rustling through the trees and I launch beams of light and love upon the breeze, knowing the wind will spread my love throughout the air and carry it to the hearts of those who need it the most.

A formula for gathering light is the daily practice of deep breathing, relaxing and releasing stress from your body. Additionally, good old fashion laughter, joy and enthusiasm are a key element to raising your light vibration. Often in our busy lives, we forget that the simple practice of deep breathing and laughing are two of the most profound abilities we possess. They are antidotes to stress. Some of you may think that you are in social media because you are trying to increase your business but I can tell you that most of you are there for the pure joy of connecting and laughing. There is not a day go by, that I don't laugh out loud to some of the things I read in my online newsfeed or while out and about shopping or traveling. It is a wonderful way to begin your day, laughing before the sun has fully risen. The world would be far more amazing if everyone began their day with laughter. Intentionally seek it out, look for something you can laugh about early in the morning; my doggies provide that joy every single day with their licks, their adorable wagging tails, their ridiculously funny antics and sweet dispositions.

"Laughter is to the soul what breath is to the body."

The Japanese have an ancient ritual which dates back approximately 800 years. Waraiko, a laughing ritual is celebrated on the first Sunday in December. Three hearty laughs are offered up during this celebration. The first is in gratitude for the passing year. The second is in prayer for the coming year. The last is for clarity and is a laugh to clear the mind and heart. In my work I have encouraged and led rituals of every kind from primordial sound, using music to create an altered state of consciousness, to washing and anointing the feet of my clients and performing light rituals an masse' with everyone dressed in white. I believe rituals are a great way to discipline the mind and create at high levels and I have also implemented laughter therapy as the Japanese do. I emphasize that laughter is as vital to the body as breath is to the soul. It is essential for good health, it is imperative for increasing the longevity of your life and it is more effective than Botox for the face. Those who laugh often and gutturally look younger than those who don't, it is just that simple.

"There is nothing comparable to the sounds of joy."

Joy and laughter go hand in hand. Laughter can actually alter your brain chemistry. Studies have shown that laughter releases endorphins and enkephalins, which help to lift mood and decrease pain. Think about that. You can diminish physical pain by laughing. The greater the laughter, the greater the release and the less you physically hurt. In my sessions with clients, I emphasize that taking your focus off of the pain and distracting the mind with enlivening activities will actually reduce the pain. Your thoughts tell your brain what to do and even the word "pain" sends a message throughout the central nervous system, the nerve endings and to the receptors of the brain, which then cause the body to react to the verbiage.

Dr. Masaru Emoto has penned several books on the power of words and their influence on water. The body is comprised of anywhere from 60% to 78% water depending on your age and gender. In his enlightening book "Hidden Messages in Water" he has photographed water when words like "hate" or "evil" are used. Conversely he has pictures of water when words like "love" and "gratitude" are used. The striking difference in how the water crystallizes or shatters with the use of negative and positive words is scientific and profound. Consequently, joy, laughter and harmonious thoughts alter the composition of the human body.

Happy thoughts whether you actually feel happy or not are elemental to shifting your consciousness. Much of what I teach is mind over matter and how to discipline your mind and reprogram your brain in order to live in harmony with all and with effortless flow. The next time you are upset, depressed, worried, fearful or just plain stressed, find a way to laugh. Go to a comedy show, tune into a TV program or rent a funny movie. When you make a concerted effort to get out of the mire and into the heart's desire, you shift your circumstance and your consciousness.

"Crying over spilled milk will not refill your cup"

When keeping a perspective in the middle of a crisis you move through it expeditiously. Wallowing in anything or harboring raw emotions is guaranteed to prolong the anguish or trauma. Staying in the problem and spending wasted energy on reviewing it or rehashing it again and again, just makes the problem appear like an unconquerable monster. Your mind becomes fixated on the problem, burying any higher solutions which are trying to flow in. Giving energy to any issue you want to relinquish, only fuels and feeds it.

Invoking laughter is the easiest thing in the world and a great way to shift your reality. People alone will give you plenty of material to laugh about. I tell you true, I laugh more at myself than anything, and like most, I often do the silliest things. I encourage others to laugh with me and enjoy self-deprecating humor. When you are confident in who you are, it is easy to laugh at yourself. I derive more joy and combustible laughter from making others laugh too and I delight in watching people react. Lifting others is my joy, I delight in it. It may sound cliché, but it is so true, that nothing cures and restores the spirit, like good, old fashion laughter.

Find a joke or story that stirs you up inside
Go see a funny movie and laugh until you cry.
For laughter is the antidote to all of life's travails
Laughing heals the body and all that it entails

Laugh with others or alone, measure not your joy
Giggle like a baby, like a child with a new toy
Laugh discreetly, laugh out loud, laugh with roaring thunder
Laugh until your sides are splitting, be not there encumbered.

Relinquish guttural release, relieve your soul to be…
Joyous, with the universe, in perfect harmony.
Fill your lungs with oxygen for laughter is an art
The benefits are endless especially for your heart.

Laugh with others or at yourself, it matters not I say
Laughter while you're working, laughter while you play
Laughter is contagious; imagine what the world would be
If everyone were laughing, in synchronicity.

"Do not become a hostage to your childhood."

There is a small child residing in every grown up; the one who lost a pet, the one who was abandoned, the one who was shy or bullied, the child who craved affection but never got it. There is a small child living in your heart, which hears and fears and falters, who longs to emerge from the darkened womb into the light of perfection; the one who just wants to be loved. That child emerges in our adulthood when we least expect it. Suddenly, as if we were back in the womb, curled up in a fetal position, our emotions unveil the wounded soul, so fragile, yet so resilient. It is in those moments we find our character and we discover our strength and our soul's ability to repair itself. It is in those moments that the spiritual seeker will turn pain into glory. Embracing the pain and allowing yourself to feel it to the bone is one way to integrate it. Then you can free it as soon as you recognize that it no longer serves you or defines you. Pain and hardship are simple reminders to go higher, to perceive with greater vision and to expand your connection to the Divine. All problems are nothing more than opportunities to tune into what you have chosen, why you have attracted, your circumstances and what you are willing to learn about yourself from all of it. You learn and grow more from adversity than you do from a problem-free life.

"Talitha cumi", the words spoken by Jesus which mean," Rise little lamb."

Children are constantly seeking new discoveries. As we age, we forget to look at the simple pleasures of life and fail to count our blessings. Every small and large element of life is a miracle in and of itself and often we forget and fail to see how very blessed we are as human beings. There are so many things to be grateful for, basic things, like the ability to breath, taste, touch and pray. Begin your own inner transformation by taking a moment right now, wherever you are, to be grateful for the breath of life and the ability to drink in the wonders of the earth and sky. Become as a small child. Be thankful for the ability to let prayer and praise fall from your lips and touch the lives of those you love. Count the blessing of your ability to taste the delectable fruits birthed from mother earth. Each day, love with every breath of your being, appreciate every fruit, every bird, every blade of grass and everything that touches all of your senses. Allow your sweetness to rise, cherish whatever brings out that pure tenderness still lurking within. Remember a time when you were blushing or giggling like a child with a new toy and be instantly transformed backwards to the days of youth, when life was kinder and gentler. Now, hold that vision and allow the tenderness to pervade you. The idea is to soften your sinews, release your burdens and allow yourself to feel a lightness of being. When you remove the emotional weight of problems and return to a state of wonder, solutions for every problem in your life can easily come to you.

"Genuine gratitude expressed will multiply your blessings."

Lightness of being is enhanced by a grateful heart. Expressing gratitude is as basic as the ability to hug someone and is essential for stepping into the dance of perfection. Return to the simplistic joys of life and ponder what a wonder you are and what a gift your arms and hands are. You are able to reach out and touch the lives of others and express love, to hold and hug furry animals and soft sweet babies.

It wasn't until I had my death experience in Austria that I realized how fulfilling a simple hug could be. I remember walking through a store and seeing a rack of fleece, feety pajamas with their enticing bright colors and the texture of a newborn lamb. I laughingly grabbed the entire rack and hugged them, rubbing my face all over the soft, billowy garments. I remember the first time I held my beautiful big tom cat and the first time I caressed and smelled a newborn furry puppy or the softness of a newborn baby.

There is nothing like touch anywhere else in the universe and when your touch is extended to others, it can be a miracle of grand proportion. A simple hug speaks volumes especially to those in need, the disenfranchised and those who have no voice, like pets and children. Your ability to hug the ones you love and strangers you meet along your journey is one of the basic expressions of the heart and many people forget just how enriching it is. When you are counting your blessings, count the ones you take for granted every day. Hugging, kissing, seeing, breathing, smelling, sensing, touching, tasting and hearing are the foundation of the human experience. As children, these are all elementary to joy. In fact, haven't you ever seen a child the very first time they taste cake or the first time they smell a flower? The wonder comes alive. In the hurry of our daily lives, many often forget these simple, yet oh so pleasurable gifts.

> *"A thankful spirit creates immeasurable prosperity and overflowing abundance."*

It's time to awaken the child within you, raise the sweetness, the tenderness, the innocence of youth again. Hug an animal, a child or an elderly person. Plant some flowers along the path of life and tend to your inner dialogue. Soften your sinews, awaken the sweet, heal the hardened soul and be born anew in love. There is so much on planet earth which enriches the soul and brings out the playfulness in all of us. Gratitude is the foundation for prosperity. The more grateful you are for the smallest blessings, the greater your blessings increase. While prosperity is a state of mind, you can literally cause more prosperity to come into your life with every grateful word you utter. Gratitude is also at the heart of purity, for the pure self in all of its essence and glory, radiates thankfulness and has a thankful heart.

"When you look at the world through the eyes of purity, you rebirth your own innocence."

I only wish that everyone could have a near death experience because you see things so differently afterwards. Everything has a vibration and an aura and suddenly the smell of coffee, the feel of fleece, the aroma of baking bread, the texture of rain on grass and your bare feet gliding across natures' plush carpet, as you run through a golden field of saffron, takes on an entirely new dimension. The earth is full of riches, textures, aromas and tastes. It is the only planet where all these fruits are laid at your feet. It wasn't until I died and left the earth, that I began to see life and its vibrancy with greater passion and while I had always loved life, my enthusiasm, my passion and appreciation increased a million times over.

I remember the very first morning following my death in the Austrian Alps. I awoke early in the morning, just in time to see the sun peeking out from behind the snow encrusted Alps. I had lived for 37 years yet had never seen how vibrant the colors of life really are. It was as if I was seeing through new eyes and smelling the delicious scents of Mother Earth for the very first time! Everything had a new vibrancy, everything including the cow manure smelled fantastic! Sadly, you don't realize it until you have left the earth but thank God I returned to be able to convey to everyone what an absolute gift life is!

Earth is extraordinary! It is a veritable buffet, a smorgasbord of delightful wonders, really enjoy it, live life with abandon and drink in all of its fruits!

Life can be so pleasurable, there's so much to explore
Life can be so bountiful, if you hungering for more.
Take a look around you now and count what's at your feet
The foods, the clothes, the plentiful, you're blessed beyond belief.

There are so many wonders, here upon this earth
Everyday sweet melodies, to enjoy for all they're worth
The smell of flowers in springtime, the taste of grapes delight
The huggable down comforter, to keep you warm at night.

The sound of wind chimes tinkling, with the lark who sings in tune
The smell of rain when falling, upon your flowers in bloom.
The touch of furry animals, which lick and love and hug
The cooing of a newborn, that at your heartstrings tugs.

The delicious taste of coffee, the aroma fills the air
The taste of sweet tomatoes, of which nothing can compare.
The visual of raspberries and cherries purple-red
The overwhelming texture and the smell of baking bread.

The twinkling of the stars as they glisten in the night
The golden glow of sunrise, as the mockingbird takes flight.

The abundance of this planet, is undervalued so it seems
Appreciate it every day and how very much it means.

Stop, see, smell, hear and taste as you absorb the delectable fruits of the earth. Give thanks for every sense you have and everything that touches them.

"Everything is created perfect, you included. All was perfect, all is perfect, and all will forever be perfect, you just have to step into Divine sweet perfection and out of the illusion."

Spiritually evolving is the road to self-discovery and self-discovery leads to evaluating everything your ego has identified as being "wrong" with you. I recently read a funny quote which said, "How to have a beach body; have a body, go to the beach!" As we age, we forget that our body is going to change and change it does. Society and its consummate worshipping of the wafer thin specimens promoted on runways and magazines have given way to self-loathing and have fed insecurities not just in women, but in men too. Well get ready, because spiritually evolving also entails many physical changes which may at times be very uncomfortable for some. While I once weighed all of 100 pounds, as I underwent spiritual processing, my body underwent radical changes. Growing, healing hang-ups, flaws, abandonment issues, betrayal issues and the like, caused some very interesting changes in my physical form and my body revealed it all at every level of evolving. Every stage of my spiritual growth offered a new anomaly. Sometimes I got thin as a rail, sometimes curvy as a whale and sometimes I even turned blue! My weight changed faster than the weather in Colorado and there were times you would have thought I lived in a third world country because I literally became skin and bones. As I gained more light and shed more of what no longer served me, as I changed my eating habits and also went through various hormonal changes, I became curvier and yes, plump like a turkey on Thanksgiving Day! There was a time when I fought it and then one day a woman said something to me which helped alter my perception. "Ariaa, I can relate to you now." I said, "Whatever do you mean?" And her reply startled me a bit, "When you were skinny, I thought you could not possibly understand me and all of my issues because as a fat women. I have been mocked and made fun of all my life. Now that you are no longer rail thin, I can actually relate to you more!"

Then another wonderful thing happened on my way to a shiny new glow. I realized one day that the more light I attracted, drank in and generated, the more I began to look like Buddha but thankfully only in the belly region. I did manage to keep all of my hair! The more light you have, the greater your increase in spiritual gifts and frankly, personal peace.

"Women come in all sizes, all shapes and all ages so there is more variety."

Whether you are on a spiritual path or not, your body will change shapes and it is high time we understand and embrace it. Your body does not define you and should never be a reason for not loving yourself.

The human body is divinely designed to accommodate the multiple chapters of your life. In your youth, you have a body built to attract a mate and create life. By middle age, you have a body made to hold your children, with enough girth to carry all your interests and activities. In your golden years, you have a form which is more fragile so that others will not focus on your form but instead on the great wisdom you have acquired and lend an ear to the infinite well of experience you have garnered. No matter what shape your body takes in between, your beauty is not predicated on your physical shell. Some of the most beautiful people in the world did not have model good looks. Conversely, some of the most physically beautiful people today often were considered ugly ducklings in childhood, including this writer.

"The greatest beauty emulates from those at peace with themselves."

The beauty that surpasses and supersedes all physical traits is the inner light existent in all, though many have dulled their glow. The more you strip away the hurts, slights, resentments, beliefs and limitations, the greater the light shines through. The greater the light, the more youthful you look, the less wrinkled you become and the more beautiful you are. Beauty is in every form of creation no matter what you look like, no matter what size your body. It's the size of your heart which defines your beauty. Beauty is innate in every creature of light and all are comprised of light. The body, mind and soul are co-dependent upon each other, if one is neglected, the other two will fail. But your outward appearance also reflects what is going on within you emotionally. How you dress, what you eat, how you talk to yourself, how you treat your body and what you feed your mind, reveal a great deal about your wellbeing. It all begins with you; you are the instrument which must be tended to, for the rest of your life to flow.

"You are the ARTIST and YOU are the canvass"

You are a masterpiece, art in movable form, a delicious blend of electric color, a unique mass of changeable form, a fantastic flow of cellular motion, an extraordinary collection of past, present and future in abstract. In you, masterworks live and breathe and add to the beauty of life. You are a direct amplification of God, a divine extension upon the earth, tracing the memory of your perfection with each footstep. If you are true to who you are, to the core of your very composition, life flows, even when things are challenging. If you forget who you are, and all the power that lies within you, you wane and your footing becomes weak, your steps skewed. You will always find your way back to the flow for it is inevitable if you are listening from within and taking heed to the whispers of angels helping to guide you. There is no separation from the Source of Light or God, unless you create one. When you still yourself and go within, you discover all the noise is your purest essence longing to be healed. The inner child and its well-being are symbiotic to the higher self. When you look at the reasons you act the way you do, respond to others the way you do and why you feel the way you feel, you begin climbing the ladder of wholeness, uncovering the joy and perfection of your being.

"Go within and glow within!"

Go higher and let the light illumine the dark spaces. Go higher and dwell in the place where ancients loom and the infinite wisdom of Divine Mind flows like an everlasting sea. Go higher and free yourself of the trappings and egos of the world, where prosperity is your divine right and love, the continuous wave you ride upon. Go higher and live inside of knowing, where all the answers come to you the moment you need them, where the roads you are intended to take come to you instead of you having to seek them out. Go higher where every thought immediately brings forth the results of your intent and the manifestations are magnificent. The imprint of mastery remains in your soul and the remembrance of all you have ever been in every lifetime, lies at the core of you. You have to seek it, you have to want to know all you have done and been. When you finally see the measure of your own lifetimes, the lifetimes where you contributed to history or created something or built something which still remains today, you integrate the strengths from those personalities and it delivers a beautiful confidence to your energy.

"At the core of every spiritual seeker there is remembrance of other roads once traveled."

Your body is the vehicle for which you carry the imprints of your most profound or impactive experiences. You carry the emotional remembrance of everything from previous diseases to strokes. Each road traveled, every path explored leaves an imprint behind, like a trail of remembrance that echoes throughout the Universe. The deeper the emotion spent at each station of life, the greater the wisdom that flows through the pools and crevasses within your body. Each memory comes with its own set of emotional and physical imprints and all are like a child, in need of nurturing and tending to. Whatever you have experienced at heighted states, whether it is fear, pain, sorrow, loss, joy, elation or any other extreme emotion, sears itself into your organs and your body, this time around. Most souls will wait anywhere between 5 to 20 years before they return to the earth. The quicker you return, the stronger the imprint of the previous lifetime and the probability you will re-imprint the old physical or emotional injury. You also hold memories deep within, of all those things which brought you joy or fear, those places where you lived before, what your craft or livelihood was, and even things like musical instruments you mastered playing in other lives.

Haven't you ever wondered about birthmarks? I remember the story of a predominant psychologist and author and his client who had come to him because her young daughter continued to tell her that, she (the little girl) was her father. At first the mother dismissed it as the ramblings of a toddler but one day her daughter began singing a childhood lullaby that only her mother and her deceased dad would have known. She was emphatic that her daughter had never heard or known about this tender moment she and her father shared during her own childhood. Stunned but open minded, she took her daughter to see Dr. Brian Weiss, a noted authority on past lives and known for his work with past life regression. In one session she found out that her daughter was indeed the soul of her dead father who had died five years before the little girl was born. The real reveal should have been obvious. The woman's daughter was born with two distinct birthmarks, one in the front and one in the back of the neck; a bullet entry and exit wound. Her father died from a gunshot wound to the neck.

Several years ago I was called to a woman's house who wanted me to lead a spiritual gathering with about twelve of her friends. Charlotte had twin, teenaged daughters and when I arrived for our first meeting, her daughter, Angela, broke into tears when she saw me. I was a bit daunted but understood what she was "seeing" energetically. It was not the first time I had gotten that reaction. She asked if she could attend the gathering and if she could bring her friend, Millie. Both girls were nineteen and both had a great interest in spiritual knowledge and of course, like many, they wanted to know about some of their own past lifetimes.

I arrived at their home the following evening, to a room full of curiosity seekers and everyone began taking their assigned seats within the half circle formation. Generally, I begin spiritual gatherings with a blessing and a prayer and then I hone in energetically and typically pull up light hearted, past life information about each person, to not only entertain, but to help them feel more empowered about their present day roles.

The gathering at Charlotte's house was proceeding along the same lines as previous gatherings when my gaze fell on Angela and her little friend Millie. Again, with an unstoppable force, words shot out of my mouth which shocked even me! I never tell someone anything which could be perceived as a negative, especially in this type of setting yet these powerful words flew from my lips! "Both of you girls take heed. DO NOT GET INTO A RED TRUCK until you have healed and cleared your karma!" I went on to tell them their names in the early 1950's, where they lived and told them that both had been white supremacists who were found guilty of dragging an African American young man behind their truck, decapitating him and they were both sentenced to the gas chamber. I warned them both that they had to heal their past life karma, which both seemed to be doing since neither was a racist in this lifetime. In fact both girls had dated other races and had multicultural friends. I additionally warned them not to be texting or messing with their cell phones while they were driving!

I counseled Charlotte and her twin girls for a couple of months when Angela decided she did not want to continue with the sessions. Her mother and sister continued to work through their issues weekly and when we felt we had accomplished what they were seeking, I completed my work with them. My goal has always been to give my clients the tools they need to continue working through their issues beyond their time with me, so I was confident they would use them wisely.

I was on the phone with another client three months later when the local news announced that Millie and Angela were driving to Kansas to visit a relative when both were killed in a rollover accident They were texting on their cell phones with a friend who was following in a car behind them. Millie was thrown from the vehicle as it was spinning in the air. Sadly, Angela was decapitated as an eighteen wheeler hit the car in mid spin, slamming it to the ground. They were driving a red truck.

Cellular memories and past life karma are not to be feared but if you are spiritually awake, you will have to address them at some point. It is a wonderful feeling when you go within and discover all you have done in other lifetimes and just how much you are capable of. In cases like Angela's you learn more about yourself and perhaps in her case that is why she embraced every race in this lifetime. Additionally you find your strengths and many times, uncover the culprit of what seem to be your unnatural fears.

You are, in and of yourself, a walking universe, comprised of every memory from every lifetime, yet most only tap into a tenth of their personal universe. It is time to awaken and behold the wonder of you coursing through every vein, every pore, and every cell of your body. Inside of you dwells the unchartered Universe waiting for the explorer to arrive. You are the sum of many lifetimes and many experiences and the composition of all these, has brought you to be the individual you are today. You have accomplished so much more than you give yourself credit for and you have overcome more than your present day circumstances. You are a walking wonder.

I was at the home of a woman who had invited me to hold a gathering for ten people but her husband was very skeptical of my gifts and frankly of me. I love a good challenge so during the evening, when it was his turn to be "read", without knowing anything about Abe Lincoln's personnel, I instantly knew this woman's husband, Len, had previously been Abraham Lincoln's secretary and even knew his name, John Nicolay! Len's, (his current name) face suddenly became white as a sheet`. His mouth dropped to the floor faster than a broken elevator. It turns out he had been obsessed with Abraham Lincoln his entire life even writing his college paper on Lincoln.

As if a fire was lit under his seat, he bolted from the room into the kitchen where Pam, our host had left her laptop computer. Within seconds he found John George Nicolay and as we all gathered around the table to read what he found, he scrolled down to the portrait of Nicolay and you could have heard the gasps ten miles away! Not only was he the spitting image of Nicolay in looks but even the clothes he wore looked like the ones in the picture of this historical figure. Len's hair and his face were exactly like Nicolay's, they looked so remarkably alike that we found it difficult to resume the gathering but now, everyone was eager to continue. After I finished reading everyone in the room to their great satisfaction, I spent about fifteen minutes in private with each person for more personal insight.

Another one of the husbands was literally shoved into the room where I was sitting by his very pushy wife, Sherry. He was clearly not a believer but upon her insistence, he reluctantly agreed to visit with me for a few minutes. He was a truck driver by trade, operating an eighteen wheel vehicle every day and on the road for weeks at a time.

Many times when I am reading someone it is as if, my mouth is motorized and I am literally unable to control what comes out of it! I blurted out, "You are about to have a heart attack within 8 days! But if they are showing me then there is time to prevent it from being fatal! You have to get to a doctor immediately!" Naturally his wife Sherry was frightened but calm because she had sensed something wasn't right with him. She inevitably promised me she would get him to the doctor the following week.

The following week came and went but on the 8th day, he was sitting in the doctor's office waiting room when he had a massive cardiac arrest! Because the doctor's office was equipped with a defibrillator and due to the staff's quick action, he survived and a few weeks later called to thank me for saving his life. Ironically, his check for the session bounced, but he came by a month later to make good on it and again to thank me. We were both relieved that we had diverted an even greater tragedy. If his heart attack had occurred while driving his mega-ton, eighteen wheeler, truck, suffice to say it could have been disastrous.

We are so much more than the naked eye reveals. I know that you know this. I am confident that each and every one of you has had one or more than one of those, "ah ha!" moments.

Perhaps it was when you were on vacation and you suddenly knew the streets or felt a strong familiarity with the country or area you are visiting or "revisiting" as it were. I also know you have all met someone who, for no apparent reason, you absolutely adored instantly or loathed instantly! Those are the memories you, as a spiritual being, are bringing to the surface. Those are the memories of the soul on the journey to remember, "Who you are." When you feel any of those unique yet unidentified emotions, ask your angels, "What is the core reason I am feeling this way?" You have to seek the answers for the answers to be revealed.

You are a walking memory bank of core lifetimes which have either helped you to evolve or have caused you to emotionally hard-set. It is not as random as it may appear. There is a divine timing to every single memory which attempts to surface. Obviously the more awakened you are spiritually, the easier it is for you to tap into that infinite well of past life revelations. Many simply run to the doctor with their various aches and pains, instead of taking a day or two to ask their angels and guides what the core reason for the physical ailment is. It is quite possible that the illness stems from current day events, emotions you are harboring or have yet to identify and deal with. But it is also possible that you are "re-experiencing" something from another time.

Clients who have dealt with knee and shoulder joint issues, have uncovered past lives where they were injured in battle or even tortured in other incarnations. Clients, who experience depression without any current day reason, have many times discovered they lost children or someone they loved to fire or some other sudden event in other lifetimes. Clients who have rage issues or issues with authority or governments often discover there are several past life incidents which created hard-set emotions and caused them to become bitter, defiant and jaded in this lifetime. Whatever the case, it is wise to look beyond the obvious in many of these areas of health and healing. Most sickness, aches and pains have a core cellular memory attached to them and are only being compounded today.

"There is nothing quite as beautiful as an emotionally healthy human being."

Sickness and "dis-ease" always have a core emotion attached to them. If you are emotionally healthy, if you are at peace with your life internally, if you do not get caught up in mass hysteria or the histrionics of the media, you will not get the flu or even a common cold. I cannot emphasize enough, how sickness is directly correlated to your consciousness and common sense or lack of it. If you go around fearing sickness or disease, of course you will attract it. It is all about balance, one foot in the heavens and one in the earth. Naturally you do whatever you need to do to treat whatever sickness or ailment you are creating but the wise will go further and ask their angels and guides to reveal in their dreams, what the core reason is for every physical anomaly.

Sickness and disease have two basic origins. Genetics do play a part but truly, sickness is derived from emotions which you have suppressed, denied or ignored, all trying to reveal themselves. The body manifests whatever you are not addressing emotionally. Any extremes in your emotional body will feed sickness and create disease unless you heal what is eating at you. Fear acts as fuel and accelerates disease, as does "fighting" the disease with anger or force of will.

In my work with clients who have low self-esteem, I begin by giving them a simple mantra, an affirmation to use all day long. If the client is insecure, I have them say to themselves and write, "I am beautiful and I love me." If they have high blood pressure I have them say, "My blood pressure is a perfect 110/70 and I am at peace with my life." High blood pressure is usually indicative of someone boiling inside, issues of unresolved anger. I know it sounds absolutely elementary but in cases like these I tell folks to "fake it till you make it," use powerful positive words until it becomes your truth. A positive inner dialogue is essential. One of my closest friends, who actually started off as a client 19 years ago, once had very high blood pressure, dangerously high in fact. She had a very difficult childhood and had severe mommy issues. Her twin was treated with loving kindness while she was ignored, demeaned or marginalized. She practiced chanting a simple mantra and was amazed to find her blood pressure had dropped to 120/80 and subsequently to 110/70 within a few short weeks.

I had another client who was always angry, chronically arrogant and absolutely hated people yet worked in a place where he had to deal with tourists every day. The very first time we spoke on video chat for his consultation, I immediately saw something in his auric field and asked, "What happened to you when you were about seven years old which emotionally traumatized you?" To which he replied in a rather angry tone, "Nothing, nothing at all!" But I never let clients off the hook that easily, so instantly, before he could even finish his curt reply I said, "It has to do with a little white dog." I was stunned when his eyes sprung a forty year old geyser and he began sobbing uncontrollably! It turns out that the core reason for his anger came down to one poignant moment in time. When he was seven years old, he and his brother were in the front yard playing when a motorcyclist came screaming down the street hitting and dragging his little white dog, never stopping. He and his brother witnessed this brutal event and needless to say, he never overcame it. It was the root to more than forty years of anger, misplaced blame and hating people, all due to that one instant, when his innocence was lost.

> **"Your body is the reactor of your emotions. It is the conduit of your thoughts."**

Everything you harbor emotionally will show up in one way or another on your body. Haven't you met people who looked older than their age because they were fraught with worry; haven't you seen someone who is angry or bitter and their face is embedded with a permanent scowl? Your body will tell you what needs healing inside, if you just listen. I could write fifteen chapters on this topic since over the years many of my clients have come to me with ailments and diseases, seeking relief and healing. I always begin with assessing what they are harboring or ruminating on. I recently had a client drop 30 pounds in four months after we addressed the anger and blame she had been carrying toward her father for more than twenty-five years. She did not diet, did not exercise and did nothing, but forgive and come to peace with her father, even calling him to make peace. She came to the awakening that she had chosen it all and took personal responsibility for the strife between them.

Louise Hay penned the definitive book on health and emotions in 1984, "You Can Heal Your Life" and I have been recommending it since its inception. In my opinion it is one of the most important books in metaphysical history. She has not only healed herself of cancers but she has helped heal thousands of people suffering from a wide range of diseases.

Again, I can't emphasize enough, how vital it is to face your own shadows and be honest with what you are feeling. The common sense factor should always be applied. Use your head, dress warm, wash your hands regularly, and get plenty of rest and vitamin C. But more, raise your consciousness and stop feeding the hysteria and fear. Stop fretting that you are going to "catch" someone else's weakness or drama. Remember the old adage, "Be careful what you wish for." The same applies with consciousness, "Be careful what you look upon, investigate or think upon, for it will indeed create."

*"Tap into the unlimited natural resources
there within your reach."*

Did you know that there are plants with healing properties?
The earth is full of untapped goods and ancient alchemies.
So many riches here to treat diseases people get
So many ways to heal human emotions that hard set.

Natural applies to health in every single way
What you eat, what you digest, evaluate each day.
Chemicals can do more harm than you can here imagine
You wake up wondering why you're tired and why your fanny's dragging.

Eat the freshest vegetables and nuts and grains and fruits
Get your protein and fish oils and do include some roots.
Taro root and other roots, some from ancient China
Can actually reverse aging while garlic helps angina.

Berries and bananas are beautiful soul food
While chocolate in small doses can improve your very mood.
Nuts and grains have fiber just like an apple every day
So many blessings in God's earth to keep sickness away.

Meditation is the natural way for you to still your mind
A way to get yours answers while your body gets aligned.
Prayer is the natural way to create at higher levels
Sleep and dreams, another way to handle life's upheavals.

Try the natural approach before you take another pill
Sleep and eat like kings and queens for that is Higher Will.
Move the mountains in your life by effective meditation
Pray for all the other things for higher elevation.

Plenty of rest, even taking a short nap in the afternoon, especially when in a spiritual process, is a great way to keep your body functioning optimally. Additionally, when you begin the day with meditation, you are not only setting your intentions for the day but you are setting the body's light ratio for the day. I have been napping for more than twenty years. I am a creature of habit and eat at about the same time every day, therefore I lie down for a half an hour right after lunch. I rarely sleep during naps but giving the body time to relax and restore is elemental to recharging your brain and the spiritual benefits are equally as elevating. Allowing time for your angels and guides to communicate is a great way to insure you develop your intuitive abilities. Additionally, you increase your light ratio and rebuild your aura every time you rest and still your mind. As an electromagnetic field, the human body is in constant motion, so lying still for a short time realigns you energetically and enables a stabilization of all five bodies of light which are typical of every human being. I have been traveling to Europe since 1991 and napping is not only common there, they actually close all the shops in many countries from noon until two o'clock p.m.! Giving your body time to restore itself just makes good sense but it also gives your angels a chance to convey whatever they may want to share with you. In my work I emphasize that my clients would be best served if they would go to bed early and awaken with the sun. It is pure synergy when you can attune your body clock to nature. The angels not only work best between the hours of 9:00 p.m. until 2:00 a.m. but your best dreams will come in those early hours of sleep.

"Plenty of sleep is essential to a perfectly functioning mind-body and soul."

How much sleep do you get when you go to bed at night?
Do you sleep right through or do you thrash 'till mornings light?
Do you make sincere attempts to go to bed quite early?
And when you don't, do you wake up feeling mean and squirrelly?

Sleep is more important than what you eat or drink,
The body requires respite to help it function and to think.
How much you need is related to your daily biorhythms,
How much you get is up to you and the lifestyle that you're living.

Meditation rests the mind and rests the body too,
Studies show that it's equal to a two hour nap for you.
But sleeping six to nine hours is the true ideal,
You know what your body needs and how rest makes you feel.

Sleep invokes the angels and offers more insight,
Into all God's kingdoms where your soul can soar, take flight.
Sleep gives organs time to rest and time to heal, restore,
Your rest is paramount to keep you healthy at the core.

In addition to good nutrition and getting plenty of rest, it is wise to be discerning of where and how you are spending your energy. Every time you step outside your door, you are subject to absorbing the energies around you. Additionally, the more activities you engage in, the more you deplete the light you gained during your morning meditation. The body requires periods of stillness in order to "reset" and "recharge" and both are accomplished by getting plenty of sleep and by practicing daily meditation. The more you meditate, the more optimally your mind, body and spirit function. As spiritual beings having a human experience, we also act as the light bearers in the world. Depending on the role you have chosen for yourself this time around, you are probably on a very evolved spiritual path, as many are. Conversely, there are those who can and will literally suck the light and life-force right out of you. Being aware of your light, your presence in the world and basically how long to stay at the fair so to speak, is essential to your own state of well-being. Being in large groups or traveling through crowded airports, anywhere where there are throngs of people, can deplete your energy, whether you are in a spiritual process or not. There are things you can do to minimize this factor such as using flower essences for psychic toxicity and showering off negative energy as soon as you are able. The primary way to maintain your body of light is simple moderation. Take the down time you need to recharge and refresh and remember that moderation is the key which opens many doors.

"Too many activities scatter energy and deplete the body."

Prompted by a client I must complete the thought,
Scattering your energy brings things you never sought.
When you spend your days in constant movement you will find,
There is no room for Spirit or to quiet your own mind.

Your body takes a hit each time you step outside your door,
You pick up other peoples moods, emotions underscored.
Pollutants, toxins in the air and harried, hurried souls,
Are counter to ethereal realms and really take a toll.

With one foot in the heavens and one foot in the earth,
You'll find that you are balanced and that balance has great worth.
Quiet time and silence can restore and heal you too,
God thrives within the silence and angels envelop you.

Prioritize your day's events and make some room for peace,
Take a nap or meditate and life will flow with ease.
Shield yourself by praying for the light to cover you,
Silence is a treasure trove and one you should pursue.

Many clients have asked me about making love and sexuality while they are in a spiritual process. When you are going through spiritual kundalini, angelic cycles or simply integrating the memories of past lifetimes, it is wise to be cognizant and protective of your energy. Spiritual processing happens to everyone based on what they chose prior to coming to Earth and everyone will go through some form or variety of spiritual processing whether they acknowledge it or not. During those life cycles, you are vulnerable and more like a sponge, absorbing all the energy of those in your life and those you encounter every day. The higher you go, the more prudent you must become or at the very least, it would be wise to do a daily meditation invoking protection and shielding yourself from negative energy.

Sexuality can be a very beautiful, spiritual interlude, but lately more people are going for the "50 Shades of Grey" variety of sexuality which is great if you are open minded. Just because you are spiritual does not negate the fact that you are human and your body is a virtual wonderland waiting to be explored. Self-respect should always be a consideration when choosing a partner for sexual encounters but when you are spiritually processing it is even more critical. You can still have wonderful, safe and satisfying sexual encounters but the key to spiritually evolving is to simply be aware of your own energy and how and with whom you are sharing it. Once again moderation in all areas of human activity produces greater spiritual balance which creates more evolution and generates greater abilities and spiritual gifts.

"Sexuality should be treated like an expensive bottle of wine. You want to share it with somebody special and savor every sip."

When you are intimate with someone, if you are a woman, you are literally taking everything your lover is emoting inside of you, into every chakra, especially during orgasm. For a woman that may also include the energy of all the women your new lover has recently been with. As you gain more light you gain more sensitivities and again, like a moth to a flame those energies are seeking light to free themselves from the darkness.

If you are a man, you actually gain more spiritual benefits from the act of intercourse than a woman does. While a woman can use intercourse to help ground her light, she must be cognizant about shielding herself from taking in any of her partners' negative energies. But a man can actually discard and expel his negative energy or frustrations through climaxing. I am in no way suggesting that you abstain from sexuality, as it is literally food for the body. However, everything in moderation is the key to your success in spiritually evolving. And choosing a lover, who you are aligned with spiritually as well as sexually attracted to, actually enhances the intensity of the encounter.

"The art of making love is sacred. Intimacy is a form of divine connection coupled with divine expression followed by divine release."

Today let's speak of passion and all that it entails,
Let's examine sexuality and any myths dispel.
I'm often ask this question, how can humans integrate,
Needs of the human body with a higher conscious state?

The answer is in knowing a balance must be found,
Between body, mind and spirit which will make the act profound.
For love must pass through mind, then energy through flesh,
Then spirit must consent to this natural request.

But understand the difference of encounters of this kind,
When trinity is captured, the results can be divine.
For flowing like a river are the passions inside you,
Making love is for the flesh, a form of earthly food.

When it's done with disregard, no thought to who you're taking,
It's then reduced from higher fields, to simple noise and quaking.
And if you take a lover who you know so little of,
You're bedding everyone to whom they've previously made love.

The energy within the art of making love should be,
Pure and effervescent delivered sacredly.
It can be very sacred, if you'll just take the time,
To choose a mate who with your soul is perfectly aligned.

The Pedestal Principle

For years I have known a simple but profound truth, which if employed, can save you from countless heartache. Our society is overwhelmed with stardom and people who are seeking their fifteen minutes of fame. We are lifting up everyone from duck hunters to dysfunctional housewives. In our daily lives, we often put stars or those who appear to have it all together, up on pedestals, disallowing the notion, that they too are human. Every human being who has ever walked this earth has made mistakes and while we label it "mistakes" the truth is, that mistakes are really nothing more than experimental living. All of life is experimental and learning is the foundation of life. It is from those living experiments that we catapult into better human beings.

I too, learned the hard way about placing people high on pedestals. I have also learned not to let others put me on an unrealistic pedestal. My personal experience has been that those who do fawn over you or over-compliment you are usually the ones who in the end, will throw you under the bus.

Years ago I was summoned to the home of a very famous actress who lived in Malibu. Arriving at Los Angeles International airport, I was chauffeured to my hotel in the very posh Brentwood area, very near where Nicole Brown Simpson and O.J. Simpson once lived. As we passed by Mezzaluna restaurant, I recalled, that it was the place where Nicole had dined with her family, on the last night of her life. That event was something none of us will ever forget.

For months those of us who are called "seers" were told by the angels, that on June 12th, the third angel would sound his trumpet. We cackled like dawdling hens, buzzing with wonder as to what the event would be. Was it an earthquake or perhaps another riot in Los Angeles? More than 8 of us, all living in different states, continued to receive the message for weeks. So it was no surprise that on June 17, 1994, we saw O.J. Simpson being driven by A. C. Cowlings, as they caravanned down the 405 freeway, with police trailing behind.

The media spectacle and the trial which followed were everywhere. There was no way to escape it. Every television station in greater Los Angeles covered every gory detail, ad nauseum. It was during the early developments of this sordid tale that the Holy Spirit literally said to me, "Stay out of it!" But how could I? It was so compelling and it permeated and saturated the air. Curiosity seekers and football fans flooded the information wheel with O.J. siting's and a torrent of propaganda. You could not go anywhere in L.A. without hearing people in the grocery stores, at newsstands and on movie sets, gossiping in wonder as to his guilt or innocence. It was a veritable feeding frenzy with the press camped out at Nicole's condo, and at 360 Rockingham, O.J.'s address, and at the Goldman's residence. Again, the Holy Spirit repeated the warning, "Stay out of it!"

Wednesday night rolled around as eight of my clients showed up for their weekly class, all wondering if O.J. did the deed. Of course being the only psychic in the room, they wanted to know what I knew. I told them that I had received an edict to stay out of it, so I could not discuss it with them, but suffice to say, I urged them to use their common sense. The answer was ridiculously transparent and we were all certain that anyone with half a brain could discern the truth.

Months went by and the trial ensued, and of course I continued to watch it despite the warnings from Spirit. The news broke in with a story from the Los Angeles airport about a reporter being attacked by A.C. Cowlings, the man who chauffeured O.J. Simpson during that famous slow speed pursuit. Apparently the reporter was going to ask A. C. about the increased level of security due to the national terrorist risk, but A.C., thinking it was about the O.J. Simpson trial, slammed the reporter up against the wall.

In that instant, seeing how violent he had become so quickly, I wondered if he had anything to do with the killing of Nicole Brown and Ronald Goldman! In my world, wondering is the same thing as seeking or asking to know the truth, and when you are fused to the Divine, anything you wonder, immediately garners a response from on high!

That night, I was inexplicably taken out of body and was suddenly in the body of a blonde haired woman, wearing a skimpy, short black dress. "We" flittered out of the side door and rounded the corner to wait for Ronald Goldman who was just about to arrive to return Nicole's mother's eyeglasses. Suddenly, out of nowhere, a large man appeared wearing a ski cap and dark clothing and "we" recognized him as O.J. Simpson. "What are you doing here?" came out of our mouth along with some other choice words. O.J. was incensed, angry and rage volatilely poured from his fists and mouth. Within minutes I felt a sting like I have never known before as he cold cocked Nicole right in the face, knocking her to the ground. Grabbing Nicole by the hair, he leaned over her body, threatening to cut the breast implants out which he had purchased for Nicole. He continued his jealous rant by telling her that he was going to cut her face in such a way that no man would ever want her again! She was terrified to the bone.

I saw another man wander onto this scene. He saw the figure of a man hovering over Nicole and I instantly knew his thoughts. He thought that a mugger had assaulted Nicole, so he began to run over to pull the mugger off of her when O.J. sprung to his feet and turned around, thrashing the air with a knife. Ronald started backing up and threw his hands up in a defensive position yelling, "HEY! HEY! HEY!"

Still in Nicole's body, "we" laid there half dazed, fully defeated. Her thoughts were of her two children who were asleep upstairs. As her entire history with O.J. flashed before her eyes, she was so afraid he would kill them. Her thoughts were my thoughts and I heard them clearly, "I knew it, he is going to kill me and Ronald and he is going to get away with it!" She had warned people for years that she feared exactly that. She had haunting premonitions that O.J. would cut her throat and get away with murder. Now lying in her own blood, she knew her fears were justified, her fate now a reality. She was helpless and could not move, dazed from the blow to her head. She was in helpless agony that she could not protect Ronald from the monster which was her ex-husband.

With Ronald killed by a stab wound to the heart and lung, O.J. swiftly returned to Nicole and grabbing her by the hair and slashed her throat from ear to ear, then dropped her as he fled. I watched as he ran to the back gate, realizing he had lost a glove, thus retracing his steps in the darkness, leaving bloody footprints along the trail. Unable to find the glove, he ran to his Ford Bronco, peeling out without turning the headlights on, almost hitting another car on the way out.

I continued to surveil the scene from the sky and I watched as he arrived home with the limousine driver waiting in the driveway. He ran around to the side of the house without being seen and changed out of his bloody clothes, falling into the outer wall of the house with a thump, all of which was brought out in his trial.

In an instant I was back in my body! I was shaking in a terror like none I have ever known. I was so completely convinced that it was me this was happening to, that I held myself in my own arms exclaiming, "It's not me it's not me, Ariaa you're okay, you're OK!!!" Her fear was my fear, her assault felt as though it was mine. I have never known such depth of terror in my life. I had gone through this horrific experience because I did not heed the warning of the Holy Spirit. While this is a very dramatic way of conveying that every thought manifests in one way or another, I think it is also an excellent way to help you understand the power of your own intentions as well.

I wrote a letter to Orenthal James Simpson, as he sat in jail and pleaded with him to tell the truth. I recited his own entire dialogue, every word he said to Nicole on that balmy, bloody night. I recounted all the details hoping to persuade him to come clean, but to no avail. The rest is as they say, history.

The Heisman trophy winning, football hero, was so publically adored, that a jury of his peers could not see what was so obvious to the rest of the world. As a society, we had elevated him and made him a god, an untouchable. Years later his fall would come, not for murder, but over the theft of his own memorabilia, for which he is currently serving a nine year sentence, in the Nevada state penitentiary.

It is normal to want to be loved and admired, but as you grow spiritually, you grow more comfortable in your own skin. The goal for all spiritual beings is to dissolve the ego's need to be fulfilled. Ego is the one absolute saboteur to all things spiritual. They are in direct conflict with each another. Those who are spiritually evolved do not need validation because once you are attuned to your inner divine nature, you are keenly aware of your own worth. Additionally, with that much power at your disposal, you become acutely aware that you must remain humble and even-keeled. Too much emotion expressed on either side of the spectrum, can trigger a dramatic avalanche.

Over the years I have fried computers, shorted out telephones and murdered televisions, all from expressing extreme emotions. Whether it is happiness or frustration, energy is just that, energy. It moves like a living creature and extends from the awakened spiritual being, as a living, life force. The old adage, "To much whom is given, much is expected," takes on a profound meaning. When you recognize the enormous responsibility which comes with living a life empowered, you open the floodgates of mastery.

The Consummate Sage

Lessons from Divine Mind

"Spiritual growth is an act of expressing divine love while procuring self-love."

As with formal education so it is with spiritual evolution. There are basic building blocks in each and those elements are the foundation you build your life upon. In spirituality, the basics should be obvious; character, integrity, honesty, self-worth, self-love, self-respect, respect for nature, respect of humans, respect for the environment, kindness, consideration, reliability, dependability, forthrightness, loyalty, compassion and empathy. These are the basic elements of the enlightened being. However, we need to also consider karma, since everything you think, say and do, returns to you multiplied. The smallest act of unkindness will bring forth more drama than you want in your life. Conversely the smallest act of kindness will produce the greatest of blessings.

"Kindness is like butter, you can never have too much of it and it needs to be generously spread on everything."

"Do no harm" needs to be the mantra of every living being and the world will know peace. When you understand that every living creation has a purpose, you realize that by killing even an insect, you disrupt the perfect balance of nature's ecosystem. But do no harm also means be mindful of your actions and how they are impacting the world around you. Think before you act, and think it all the way through. Take a moment to assess what all the possible outcomes of your actions would be, even the farthest fetched ones. Take a moment to pause and evaluate what the consequences of each choice will be, because there are always consequences. When you remove the emotional aspect and take time to really think your reactions through, it makes an enormous difference in how you live your life. Live deliberately, not impulsively.

Tenacity and resilience are two of my favorite elements to building good character. That's because my star students and clients have been those who plowed through the difficult challenges awakening entails and kept going, despite how emotionally uprooting it was. Being tenacious, runs akin to resilience because those who persevere are typically very resilient. Resilience is also critical to spiritually evolving since you have to keep going even through the most difficult of days.

When evolving spiritually, you also have to be patient as every memory, every process and every step you take up the tree of life, is precisely orchestrated. Once you begin to see the tangible evidence of your spiritual labor, you begin to hunger for more! There is nothing more gratifying than having the instant knowing and insight of what direction to take in your life, or the ability to pray and have that prayer suddenly become a reality. There is nothing more enriching as having a vision or dream of something yet to come and the great satisfaction that comes, from praying for perfect strangers in advance of world events.

> *"To touch the heart is beautiful ...to touch the soul ...eternal."*

For me, there is nothing as enriching as helping people to heal themselves and transform their lives. I have seen the most amazing transformations in thousands over the years and at each new level of consciousness I personally ascended to, there were new gifts and benefits to bless others and those in my life. The greatest blessings bring immense joy, like seeing clients healed of fibromyalgia after only a few sessions or seeing them withdraw naturally from prescription drugs after years of usage because they were given the tools needed to tune into their soul and access the answers which healed them. The smaller blessings also offer a window into how well you are creating. You know you are blessed when the first parking space opens up during a major blizzard or when arriving at the market. That is divine flow! Having an internal alarm go off when your are near someone who is dangerous or having your cell phone carrier agree to let you out of your contract with a year left on it without a financial penalty, now that really is flow!

> *"If it doesn't flow, let it go."*

I tell you that in jest because most people go through life in a constant state of struggle. Many don't even realize what being in the flow is like and how liberating it is. Many fight against the unseen river flowing through life every day and often because of something as simple as pride, ego and fear. The flow is always available but you have to invite it in or step into it. The flow is the highest will for your life and when you surrender to it, even when things go awry, there is a peace and knowing within you that lends itself to the certainty that all will work out fine. But there is one drawback, you have to surrender at times when you want your way but your way is not necessarily in the flow. The key is remembering that there are many variables to creating and some you cannot see, so it is best to check your ego at the gate and make sure you are diligent and specific in what you are trying to create. Use the "I am" or the "I have" to create what you want as if you have it already. Then know that you know that you know and don't let anything diminish or tame your vision.

Many times the answers are right in front of us and they come in ways we least expected. I am a firm believer in the notion that everything comes to us at just the right time. In fact one of my favorite quotes is a Buddhist proverb, "When the student is ready, the teacher appears." Often divine messengers are the neighbor passing by or a stranger who strikes up a conversation with you at the grocery store. Many folks are looking for lavish, over the top displays but remember Spirit speaks in the still small recesses of your mind and heart. Learning how to listen with an open heart and spiritual ears is essential to developing your higher self and increasing your spiritual gifts. Listening and hearing are two different things. How do you receive what those in your life are saying? Do you hear with an open heart or do you hear through veils of subterfuge? Do you wait for the other person to finish speaking or do you anticipate their answer, ready to jump in with your own thoughts?

In clinical studies at the University of Missouri, it was tested and shown that immediately after listening to a ten minute oral presentation, the average listener heard, understood and retained 50% of what was said. Within forty-eight hours, that dropped off to 25%. In other words, we often comprehend and retain only one-fourth of what we hear. Another reason for poor listening skills is that we think faster than most people speak. Most of us speak at the rate of about 125 words per minute. However, we have the mental capacity to understand someone speaking at 400 words per minute.

For the spiritual traveler we see things a bit more expansively. For example, what is your heart's capacity to hear? Are you nursing old patterns and old beliefs which muddy the waters and prevent you from hearing what is truly being said? Are those same patterns preventing you from hearing solutions which could help balance your life and heal your issues?

In my practice, I sometimes see couples who are experiencing problems in their relationship and many times it comes down to the way they communicate. I often find that they are hearing with a chip on their shoulder or through the eyes of a wounded heart which then skews the message. Emotional barriers such as hurt, resentment, lack of forgiveness or anger, act as a block to higher solutions. Additionally, one of the things I emphasize most in my work is learning to hear your inner dialogue so you can weed out culprits like heartache, low self-worth or old beliefs which taint the way you interact with others. When you are internally verbally bashing yourself and nursing the dysfunction, you hear from that very perspective. There is a quote from an unknown source which reads, *"If someone in your life talked to you the way you talk to yourself, you would have left them long ago."* Hearing what another person has to say, not only in your personal relationships but in everyday life, is critical to expanding your sense of compassion and caring. Everyone on this planet has a built in need to be loved. Listening to another human being is one way to convey that feeling.

"We are all connected, what you do affects everyone around you, even the lives of total strangers"

I was in New York City to sing at the United Nations and we took a day to visit the Metropolitan Museum of Art. It was October, cold, raining and wet, yet as we pulled up, I noticed a beautiful coiffed elderly lady, dressed to the nines, standing in the rain holding her umbrella as if it were a regal scepter. Even though it was pouring and my feet were soaked to the bone, I had to know; I could not let this chance pass me by to engage pass me by. I walked up and paid her a compliment which couldn't have been more sincere. I was stricken by her inner beauty which glowed outwardly. I was intrigued at who she was in the grander scheme of things and why I felt so drawn to her.

Her name was Mary and as she spoke you could see she what her life must have been, so proud and stoic. She had a unique story to tell. Like the glistening drops of rain, she began pouring her life out almost as if she was about leave this earth and just needed one more person to know that her life amounted to something. I stood there listening, my heart began to well up inside and tears ran down my cheeks. I tried to nonchalantly brush them away as I listened for it was a profound tale indeed, better than a juicy novel. She married the love of her life at the end of the great depression and then war came and her new husband was suddenly shipped overseas. She was left alone with two babies to raise, twins who were barely two years old. She worked for the USO and took a typing job on the side to make ends meet until her husband returned home a few years later. Together they raised ten children and every one of them decided to go into the field of law and criminal justice. Six of them were successful lawyers, while the other four were police officers, including her only daughter who sadly was shot and killed in the line of duty. She continued weaving the intricate details of a life rich and full and as she spoke her eyes wandered to the sky as if to be whispering a prayer. She never shed a tear as she unveiled and bared her soul to me, I could feel her engorged heart so full, yet dignity forbade its implosion. The rain continued to beat down but I never felt a drop because I was so consumed in her life and the majesty of her grace, the way she articulated herself with such pride. Thirty minutes later, her ride arrived. We hugged and I asked if I could take a picture with her which of course she obliged. We hugged again and then departed. Despite the fact that I was visiting one of the world's greatest museums, it was the best thirty minutes of the day.

I tell you in my travels around the world for more than twenty-two years, I have had many such experiences. In my volunteer work with the elderly, many times I just sit and listen to the stories of their lives. Life is so much more enriching when you get out of yourself and see the world through another's eyes. Engage often with those you meet along your journey, you never know how full your heart will become until you have loved a stranger by walking in their shoes.

> *"Be kind to strangers for you never know what they have overcome in their lifetime."*

Everyone has a story and I love and thrive on the rich texture of people and all they have to offer. Every single soul has their own perceptions, reactions and vivid remembrances of all they have experienced. When you take the time to learn from the very strangers you pass by every day, you expand your own humanity.

One of the reasons I feel social media has become so essential in society is that all of us want to share our stories, our gifts, our challenges, our heart. Most of us thrive on the connections and grow from the depth of what we learn from each other. I know my own life is enriched by connecting with souls from every culture and every nation. Most of us want an avenue to be heard, to extend ourselves into a growing world where communication is imperative in designing our future. For years now in social media I have posted, "Have I told you how much I love you, how much you add to the depth and breadth of my life…I will," and I mean it with all my heart. There is nothing quite as enriching as hearing inspirational stories which compel all to have more courage, strength and perseverance.

We all want to connect, it is innate, it is essential. Often we forget that everyone we pass is a culmination of their own movie board. People tend to go through their day with blinders on never noticing the people around them. If you look closely you'll see opportunities to make a difference with the smallest gesture. You don't have to give in a grand display, for it is the little moments in life that comprise the whole. You can give a simple compliment to a mother who is struggling to make ends meet, who has lost the remembrance of her beauty or to an elderly man wandering through a store longing for his heyday when he was not overlooked by society. A kind word or a smile to a child whose face wears the emotional scars of the fights his parents are having or an uplifting word to a woman going through a bitter break up who has just been betrayed and is full of hurt, makes all the difference in the world. How will you find these people? It's simple, look all around you, they are everywhere. I ran into a woman at the grocery store who lost her home to the worst fire in Colorado's history, the Black Forest fire, and I did not hesitate for a second to grab hold of this traumatized woman to hug and hold her as she wept.

"Sit up and take a genuine interest in a fellow human being...it may just be an archangel you are entertaining."

Everyone you pass has a story, has a woe, or has been wounded in some way. You can touch a life with a simple gesture of kindness, a hug, a dollar, a compliment, lending a hand or an uplifting word. I have often found that the smallest acts of selflessness are the ones which leave a lasting imprint on the soul.

I hope to inspire you to listen, observe and participate in the world around you. Look up when you're walking through the streets or store. Make eye contact, smile, talk to the man in line next to you or the mother holding her infant, counting her change. You could very well be the instrument the angels are placing there at that very moment, to lend a shoulder to someone in need, when all the while you thought you were just going to the store.

"You can learn a lot more by listening than by talking. Hearing with open ears and an open heart can produce greater learning than an entire set of encyclopedias".

Stop and listen, can you hear, the voice that calls aloud
Stop and listen to what is found, far from the maddening crowd.
Hear the voice inside your heart, it whispers sweet and low
Hear through veils of subterfuge, to the depths within your soul.

Listen to the man who speaks in whispers as he walks
Listen to the woman there unto herself she talks.
Listen to the crying child outside your windowsill.
Listen to the elderly, they've so much to reveal.

Hear the voice of your best friend with guidance clear and true
Hear the voice of your enemy and learn what not to do.
Listen to the newscaster who reports the day's events
Hear with your compassion, care for those whose lives are spent.

Hear the loneliness inside of that woman passing by
The one you never noticed had a tear within her eye.
Listen to the overweight, for many times they'll be
Hiding from the world in shame, their worth they just can't see.

Listen to the longing of the teen that's been betrayed
Listen for they'll tell you of themselves they are afraid.
Hear the disenfranchised, from all across the globe
Hear the ones who have no home and no place they can go.

Hear your guides and angels for many dwell within the earth
Listen to the teachers who've made teaching their life's work.
Listen to the signs from God, for signs are everywhere,
Listen for they'll guide you, you are reading one right here.

There is another grand advantage to listening. You can avoid a lot of unnecessary heartache by listening with a spiritual ear because people will always show you who they are when you first meet them, if you are paying attention. We tend to perceive people the way we want them to be instead of the way they are and while giving people the benefit of the doubt is good, you have to exercise the spiritual gift of discernment. Discernment is one the tools the masters teach as being instrumental to evolving your consciousness. Webster's Dictionary describes discernment as, the quality of being able to grasp and comprehend what is obscure or an act of perceiving.

*"Remember what a person shows you
the first time you meet them."*

I had an oral surgeon many years ago and one of her closest colleagues kept warning me that she was a "sexual predator." Naturally I was shocked by his admonition and I was pretty sure he was being harsh because she had probably rejected his advances. Boy was I wrong. It was 2004 and I was very naïve and clearly suffering from a severe lack of spiritual discernment. In hindsight I look back on the very first "personal conversation" we had where she revealed that she had been having an affair with her husband's best friend, who just happened to also be a dentist. She laughed as she told me of their sexual trysts and how they had even slept together in the house she and her husband shared, with her children sleeping right across the hallway! Instead of running for the hills, I naively remember thinking that maybe I could help her. After all, it was my line of work. I thought with a little counseling and perhaps giving her a new perspective on karma and honesty, that she would surely change the course of her deceptive path. It wasn't long before I saw firsthand, what those earlier signs had tried to tell me. She told me in that first conversation that she could not be trusted, that she had no moral compass and that she relished in deceit. She showed me in that instant, that she would have her way, no matter who it hurt, including the father of her children, her children, her lover's wife, and those they loved.

You see, I was listening but I listened through a filter instead of actually hearing what should have been obvious. Suffice to say I learned a very valuable lesson as she proceeded to undo my own personal life. She caused heartache and chaos while accompanying me and my husband on our annual trip to Germany and Austria. With a predatory nature, she poisoned everyone she touched in two countries. I have never met a more toxic human being.

In just one monumental event, I mastered the art of discernment. It was one of the most painful experiences I have personally encountered but as I teach it, I also live it. I used this traumatic ordeal as a catalyst to catapult higher, and have since learned to pay attention to the signs. There are always signs. I recognized and owned that I had attracted this scenario to expand my consciousness and to learn to listen with a greater awareness, as well as fine tune the principle of discernment.

All lessons on the road to illumination are unfortunately painful, but if you move through them expeditiously, you gain greater light and your spiritual gifts are greatly increased. The key, as with any good lesson, is to learn it the first time around.

"When others show you who they are, trust it."

Too many times we fail to honor what our gut is telling us and overlook or ignore that gnawing feeling inside trying to guide us. It may be trying to keep you from danger or perhaps trying to steer you away from a toxic person or situation, as was the case with my oral surgeon. Your gut feeling is the inner knowing, the higher self and the pure Divine mind which lies inside of every human being. Learn to pay attention to the subtle signs, to fine tune your inner knowing, and act upon it, instead of ignoring that inner guidance and regretting it later.

When you look at someone, do you see beyond the surface? When you speak to another person do you hear what they are saying, or do you actually listen to how they are saying it, hearing the emotions in their words? When you read an email, card, letter or social media post, can you "feel" what you are reading? Everyone has a sixth sense and everyone has the ability to "tune in" and to go beyond the obvious, to the sublevels of consciousness in people. When you see beyond the veil and when you look deeper into the hearts of others, many times that essence will guide you in knowing, whether to engage further or to distance yourself.

"Be aware friends will come and go, let them."

Haven't you ever met a stranger waiting to become your friend, who spilled out their secrets without reserve, revealing their character or lack of it? Haven't you seen social media posts, which made you gasp, cringe or even cry? Most people will show you who they are within, minutes, hours or a few days of meeting them. If you listen, they will reveal their character, their emotional baggage, their mental or physical issues and their mindset. If you really tune in, people will show you who they truly are. Are they consistent in what they say and do? Do their words have depth or are you hearing or reading the same shallow sentiments each time they post? Are you easily fooled, are you connecting with people who will drag you down to their level? Or, are you attracting those who will take you to a higher evolution, to a new plateau of growth? Recognize that who and what you support, or form attachments with, will either enhance or dim your personal light and could malign your character.

Today, I urge you to take an intuitive walk through your interpersonal circles and see if you have surrounded yourself with those of high character or those who have little to none. It can be the difference between a life filled with drama or one of divine flow. For all intents and purposes, your gut is God. You are the expression, the amplification of the Creator light with all the answers right inside of your very being. Stop to listen to the perfect rhythms of your mastery within.

The first time that you meet someone tread carefully, assess
How they act and what they say, to you what they confess.
Many times we overlook the things that people say
Many times people reveal inconsistencies at play.

We often will dismiss those things as trivial or trite
What we feel deep in our gut is probably what's right.
We sometimes question ourselves asking if we're being hard
We often doubt our own instincts, our feelings disregard.

In my life experience I've learned my gut is God
I've learned to heed the warnings whether normal or quite odd.
I've learned to watch and listen when another person speaks
So often you will clearly see where truth wanes or leaks.

The smallest indiscretion should tell you to go slow
The smallest acts of deceit reveal all you need to know.
If someone will deceive and lie to the souls they love
What makes you think you're different or that you'll be thought more of.

It isn't that you stand as judge and hang them with aplomb
But what you hang around with you surely will become.
What you lend your heart too will soon become your cage
When you meet this kind of soul it's best to turn the page.

Today remember that first impressions are rarely inaccurate.

"When answers can no longer be found outside, divine solutions unfold inside."

Throughout the annals of time psychologists and scientists have tried in vain to define "intuition." According to the renowned neuropsychologist Roger Sperry, "Intuition is a right-brain activity while factual and mathematical analysis is a left-brain activity. The reliability of one's intuition depends greatly on past knowledge and occurrences in a specific area. For example, someone who has had more experiences with children will tend to have a better instinct or intuition about what they should do in certain situations with them." It has been said, that Swiss psychologist Carl Gustav Jung's analytical psychological theory of synchronicity, is equal to intellectual intuition. Jung concluded that intuition is perception via the unconscious in the spiritual world.

Intuition is a knowing, a sensing that is beyond the conscious understanding, it is a gut feeling. That "gut feeling" is your higher self. Your "higher self" can be defined in many ways; it is the pure essence of you, free of ego, free of judgments, free of any limitations, free of dogma or belief systems. The higher self is also known as the Super Conscious Mind or Divine Mind.

Divine Mind makes all things you conceive a reality in the physical world. Many call that God, Creator, Spirit, the I AM presence. You may call it whatever you like because it's semantics. The Super Conscious is another way of saying "the Source of light" or "the Source of quantum love" from which everything else emanates. When you shut out the noise, sit in complete silence and tune into the source of pure love within you, answers to every question can be ascertained. Now clearly during the course of your day, you are not walking around in a meditative state but as you learn to fine tune your gut feeling, it becomes more first nature in every area of your life. The mind has to be tamed to get out of the way of your gut instinct and once you learn to tune into that feeling, you'll typically find it is always spot on. Intuition's worst enemy of course, is intellect and rationalization. Your mind or ego is in a constant battle with your higher spiritual gifts, with your higher self.

"Self-confidence and ego are exact opposites, one comes from knowing, the other from not."

Years ago, my husband was working for a very large corporation and one of the perks was a company car. After having a new van for a few short weeks, something suddenly told me to have the brakes checked on the vehicle. That something was my intuition. With a typical left brain response, my husband did not miss a beat. His ego launched into an argument about how the company would never pay for unscheduled maintenance on a brand new van. Despite knowing my spiritual gifts, he stubbornly refused to take the car in to have the brakes checked. We lived in Sedona at the time and the only place to have the work done was 16 miles away in Cottonwood.

The next day we drove north 30 miles to Flagstaff and later that evening, my angels and guides chided me and insisted that I stay out of that van until the brakes had been checked. The next morning, I woke up and insisted Michael take the van to Cottonwood to have it checked, which he begrudgingly did.

Four hours later he returned to the house and when he walked through the front door, he was as white as a sheet, looking like he had seen a ghost! I was startled by the look on his face and when I asked what was wrong, he began tearing up and he was not the kind of man who openly showed his emotions. He began to tell me that when they put the van up on the lift, they found a defective Firestone tire with an enormous bubble ready to explode, but it was located inside, where it would not be seen unless you actually removed the tires to check the brakes. Many of you may remember the Firestone tire recall in 2000. Experts believe as many as 250 deaths and more than 3000 catastrophic injuries were associated with the defective tires. My husband went on to say, that the mechanic told him that two weeks earlier a couple had been killed in the same style van, in a rollover accident with the very same issue. It was identical in every way. The back tire had exploded causing the driver to lose control of the vehicle. Listening to my intuition saved us from the same fate.

"The whispers of your heart speak louder than your words"

Last summer, I rushed like I was on fire through Wal-Mart as if

I were in a race and did not understand why. Minutes after I walked out the door before I was even in my car, a man fired gunshots into that very door. I had literally dodged a potential bullet, once again, because I honored my gut feeling and did not question why I was compelled by such a hurried energy.

I can recite countless times when my intuition has literally saved me. I even recall a dream I had many years ago which included one of my clients at the time. I dreamed that it was snowing wet, heavy snow, earlier in the year than usual. In the dream I was screaming, "Call 911 Call 911!" I was standing with my client in a building and in the dream I knew, it was a warning of impending danger. I was shown other things too, as if I was supposed to connect the dots.

The next day I phoned the client and told her about my dream and that I felt one or both of us were in danger. I informed her that all precognitive dreams occur within 48-72 hours, so we needed to be diligent for the next few days. She agreed and on the third day, we both awoke to an unexpected, wet, heavy snowfall. My husband and I had to travel to Denver which was about an hour from our home that morning. I was really concerned but as I live my life, I was unafraid. As we drove to Denver, the snow began to clear and the sun came out! I was thrilled and thought something must have shifted because the roads cleared and we drove without incident to our destination. We took care of our business in Denver and headed back onto the highway for the long drive home in afternoon traffic. Soon there was a clearing and I found myself going well above the

75 MPH speed limit, which is not my typical way. I was driving a brand new car and still had not adjusted to the touchy gas pedal, when suddenly, with no explanation the car's ignition literally turned itself off! As I wrestled with the power steering trying to pull over to the side of the road on a very busy freeway, I was horrified! I could feel the danger approaching but was sure that since the angels had forewarned me, we were going to be fine. I managed to get the car onto the shoulder of the freeway and tried to restart it but it simply would not start! My husband was about to get out of the car when I looked in the rear view mirror to see an 18-wheeler barreling down the hill and it looked as though he was coming right at us! I told Michael to brace himself and I closed my eyes. We braced for impact and began to pray and then…whoosh! The oversized truck swerved around us and missed us by a wing and a prayer! We breathed a deep sigh of relief and I tried to start the car again and to my surprise it started with ease! It was in that moment I knew. I knew that we were going to encounter an accident up ahead and that we would have been involved in it, if not for the car turning itself off. Sure enough, at the very exit where my client lives, there was a seven car fatal accident which killed two people. Call it angels, divine intervention or whatever you wish, but the fact remains, that if the ignition had not turned itself off, I would have surely been involved in that accident.

I have honed this skill over the years and have learned to listen and act when my gut speaks to me. I can tell you story after story where my intuition has saved me from circumstances that would have been dire. It works in everyday, simple matters too such as with timing, being at the right place and the right time to avoid traffic, lines, delayed flights, or anything else you apply it to.

> *"Your gut feeling is always accurate and when you practice paying attention to those innate feelings, you improve the quality of your intuition".*

Intuition may be defined as understanding or knowing without conscious recourse to thought, observation or reason. Some see this unmediated process as somehow mystical while others describe intuition as being a response to unconscious cues. Some even see it as angels guiding them. What I wish to emphasize is the fact that intuition cannot be negated. Time and time again we hear about mothers who are so attuned to their children, that they know instinctively when something is wrong. We've have all seen stories of how a person's gut feeling kept them from boarding an ill-fated airplane or how intuition paid off for those who had a gut feeling to suddenly play the lottery.

Intuition and telepathy are symbiotic and work well when orchestrated together. Telepathy is the skill of honing a thought and deliberately projecting it to another person, in order to accomplish communication when logistics is an issue. Many times it is random while some like me, practice this wonderful truth principle for a multitude of spiritual purposes such as healing, creating or comforting another.

In the days of the Essenes in ancient Judea, there was such a perfect harmony in the culture that one could think a thought and another in the community would act upon it. An Essene woman could be out in the field harvesting the crops and think, "I need to breastfeed my child" and instantly, that loving thought, would travel telepathically to one of the other mothers in the community who would simply pick up the baby and nurse it.

Today, we are returning to this kind of oneness, this kind of a spirit of cooperation and harmony. Your participation in escalating and elevating the love within you is not only welcomed but highly appreciated by those of us who practice intuition and telepathy. The possibilities are endless when you consider how much humankind could resolve, if we all heightened our telepathic capabilities and would attune and polish our own intuition.

"In a world of ordinary, why wouldn't you choose to be extraordinary?"

You ask, "How do I learn to tune into my intuition and how do I develop my telepathy?" It's easier than you think. It is a matter of discipline and learning to read the most subtle energies. You've heard the phrase "a woman's intuition" and indeed women are better at intuition due in part to sensitivities and because women are more in touch with their emotions and feelings. Women pay more attention to those details, and by mere virtue of being mothers, have a heightened sense of awareness.

Meditation is one definitive way to learn how to hear that still small voice within because your gut is God. Meditation is also a good tool when learning how to decipher your gut feeling and separate it from intellectualizing or from other fears which may alter your perception. Recently a client ask me how to know if you were on the highest path for your life and the answer is, your gut will tell you when you're not.

Like intuition, mental telepathy is innate as well and whether you realize it or not, you practice it more often than you think. It's that moment when you think of someone and they suddenly phone you or you sense your child has been hurt on the playground only to discover you were right. You send thoughts out every day and telepathy is the art of transmitting with deliberate intention as opposed to allowing your thoughts to be random. Thoughts as we all know, are energy and intention propels the energy. So when you direct the thought to someone, depending on how receptive they are, the thought is received. This morning I was in the shower and started thinking about an old boyfriend and sure enough, two hours later, he phoned to say hello. You can use telepathy to reach people, the help others or to improve the quality of your own life.

Let me just articulate a summation of this realm,
I heed my intuition like a driver at the helm.
In this world of ordinary life can be so surreal,
In this world of mystical it's what you sense and feel.
When the Source of pure love speaks within your heart,
When angels whisper wisdom and intellect departs.
Answers unfold quickly when tuned to the Divine,
Listen to the voice within its speaking all the time.

"Raise your inner dialogue then you can raise the world."

Telepathy and intuition, like all spiritual gifts, have to be practiced to become polished and effective. By improving your inner dialogue, the way you talk to yourself and the messages you allow to roll around in your head, you improve the quality of these tools. Seek to use words which uplift, motivate and inspire yourself and others. Seek to raise your own inner dialogue, be kind and gentle with yourself, but take yourself to task and address and heal the unnecessary emotional baggage. In doing so, you elevate your frequency which in turn, unveils your higher gifts or spiritual tools. By disciplining your emotions your free your psyche to evolve.

What are you creating with your behavior every day?

What are you empowering in the things you think and say?

What do you put in the world which boomerangs right back,

Do you feel the victim to your own karmic attack?

Do you blame the world around for what comes back to you,

Or do you see your thoughts and words just multiplied and grew?

The way you treat those in your life,

The things you say and think

Will be the measure of your life, the well from which you drink.

Rid yourself of anger, forgive with ease, stop nursing old hurts and limited beliefs which tie you to misery and bind you in darkness. Seek to love softly, silently, loudly with passion, to love yourself and others with kindness, tenderness, compassion but with the force of a thousand angels enveloping the earth. Remove the blockages which prevent your higher gifts from shining through. Seek to become the vessel that light shines through, the instrument that love overflows from. Be born anew with the realization, the recognition that you have more power inside of you than you know. Discipline your mind. Let it become a constant stream of messages which uplift you and the world around you.

"Your inner dialogue creates your outer reality."

Why feed the negatives you hear on the news or from the gossip of others or those in your life? You choose what you allow yourself to buy into. Why buy damaged goods? Why do you rerun those childhood comments your teachers, your parents, your siblings or the school bully said? Most relive those painful moments without even realizing that inner dialogue is the very thing which is sabotaging your current day dreams.

You can use your thoughts like biofeedback and empower and heal yourself with more effective thoughts which you deliberately set into motion. You have more power inside you than you know and telepathy is a real art form. Thoughts are energy and the more you learn to use your telepathic mind to create, the greater your gifts increase. Don't just watch your words, formulate your thoughts to make a difference. With enough energy propelling it, what one thinks becomes so and creates a ripple effect in life. Thoughts are power, words are power, all is energy, use it wisely. You can heal yourself and you can be filled with so much love, the excess pours out on all creation.

***

"The greatest love affair you will ever have is with yourself."

One of my greatest passions is helping people learn how to love themselves. In my practice I have seen everything from drug addiction to chronic illness to physical abuse and more. The variables can be genetic, environmental, karmic and socio-economic but no matter what they are, always without exception, a lack of self-worth, self-respect and self-love are at the core.

Loving yourself can be the difference between a life of flow or living a life filled with dramas. It is no secret that self-worth and self-esteem are essential but many people fail to connect their lack of self-love to something they did in a previous lifetime. I guide my clients by first assessing this lifetime and what their childhood experiences are, then we delve deeper. Many times you are carrying memories of something which traumatized your spirit, your body or your psyche from another time, a previous incarnation. There are many ways to uncover events which happened long ago but many only focus on their current lifetime. Those who have reached higher levels of conscious flow are those who have explored every pillar within. In other words, look deeper, go higher, seek from within and with the help of your angels and guides, uncover what haunts your spirit. It may simply be from your own childhood but whatever the reason...

"Nothing thrives where self-love lacks."

One way to raise self-love is to feel your fears, then heal your fears. Fear is energy capable of sabotaging your dreams and it certainly veils the love which resides at the core of your being. When you fail to address what haunts you, it grows and feeds from your neglect to tend to it. Fear must be embraced to understand it, the parameters must be scoured to find the core of your fear. The more you push it away, the more you attract what you fear. Discovery is half the lesson. In your search, you will often find that the thing you fear, is only a by-product of something fixable and most of the time it is self-love and having more faith. When you love yourself there are no constraints, no limits and there is no hindrance to the joy you encumber and express. Faith is self-love in motion and you must have faith in your higher self to manifest all you dream. Faith is a potent powerful energy. God, Spirit, the I Am presence and the source of all creation is unlimited. It is your divine composition and when you tap into god-power, when you activate that god-knowing, there is nothing you cannot accomplish. When you love yourself, you experience life with a passion unstoppable by anything including fear.

"Fear is a dam which paralyzes divine flow."

Most who wrestle with love and insecurity are riddled with fear inside. The fear of not being accepted, not being good enough and the fear of failing are crippling, but when you address the fears and confront them, you usually discover that there was nothing to fear at all.

Consider South Africa's the lion whisperer, Kevin Richardson, who plays, sleeps and lives with wild lions, hyenas and other "predators". Consider Jane Goodall, British primatologist, ethnologist, anthropologist, and UN Messenger of Peace. She is considered to be the world's foremost expert on chimpanzees, which many consider very dangerous. Consider the monks of Tibet who live amongst wild tigers in India and Nepal. In my own life, I hand fed a pack of four wild boars on a regular basis while living in Sedona. I have hand fed snakes, marmots, chipmunks, lamas, goats, raccoons, squirrels, giraffes, elephants and other creatures who most think will bite you or spit at you and the truth is, they will, if your heart is not in the right place and your frequency is not attuned to love. Animals and nature alike can feel and sense love and fear in human beings and they react accordingly. Animals, like humans, are a cosmic mirror to your own soul and whatever you are feeling they emulate.

Haven't you ever known someone who is chronically sick or perhaps suffers from neurosis or psychosomatic illness? If you look at their pets, you will see a similar pattern, animals that are always sick or have behavioral issues. If you look farther, you can always tell what is going on in the household by observing the pets in the house.

Whether there is fighting, anger, sorrow, sadness or joy and harmony in the house, the pets will wear it like a scarlet letter. It is similar to what humans feel as you encounter them in your everyday life. We attract whatever we are emotionally nursing. Those you draw to you will also be full of fear and insecurity when you are not certain or confident in who you are. Not only do others feel and sense your insecurities but they will have an aversion to it and repel you most of the time, just to avoid the cosmic mirror and dealing with their own self-love issues.

"Loving yourself is the great connector to all things divine"

When you fail to love you, you are incapable of loving others fully and they will have a very hard time staying in a friendship or relationship with you. You are also negating the Creator Light because everything created is an extension of the Omnipotent Light of God and everything which stems from that light, was, is, and will always be perfect.

We are returning to love, to balance, and are reawakening the "kind" in humankind. When you address those anomalies which veil you and prevent more light from shining through your soul, you raise your own vibrational frequency and it is very tangible. Animals and humans can feel what you are emitting.

"Love is the great denominator the great neutralizer and the great elevator."

Love is all consuming, capable of neutralizing every other emotion within you. But more importantly, love is the quantified composition of the Source Light from which you are born. The purer your spirit, the nearer you are to the core or Source. The nearer to the Source you become, the greater your abilities increase and the greater your life flows on Earth. Pure does not mean you have to be a saint, it simply means you are implementing love and putting kindness into action. It takes a great deal of discipline to stay in a heart of love but with practice it becomes first nature because it IS first nature, you are comprised of divine love. Now imagine that kind of omnipresent love translating to all humans. When you make yourself a pure vessel of love, when you heal the ravages of old hurts, slights, betrayals and heartaches, the pure essence of you is revealed and you emit a frequency so loving, others are transformed by your light, by your very presence.

"When you elevate your frequency to the perfect rhythms of love nothing will harm you."

Additionally, projecting your fears and anger crosses universal law and is a guaranteed way to ensure a quick karmic return. Anger attracts negative forces faster than any other emotion because of energy and intention. Intent is how the universe sees you. When you fail to address what is hurting you on the inside, it begins to build and often explodes as rage onto others. When you regurgitate your emotions propelling them at others, it is a form of abuse. That's right, you are verbally assaulting others, each time you scream or yell and it matters not if it is directly or indirectly at others. The normal decibel range of human speaking is about 50 decibels but when a human is screaming or yelling it can exceed 80 decibels which can shatter the human aura, damage the ear drum, and rattle the central nervous system.

When you fail to take personal responsibility for what you are feeling and why you are feeling it, you miss the entire purpose for living which is to grow and master human emotion. Not only is anger dangerous, but unhealed it can lead to depression, it will shorten your lifespan and can lead to addiction and certain diseases like cancer.

"Anger like alcohol, strips away the veils and reveals the core character of a human being."

There are innumerable ways to heal anger, I urge you to seek them and stop allowing your emotions to assault those you love. One way is to take the person you are angry with and in your head turn it around. For example, let's say you are mad because your husband came home late for dinner, a dinner you spent hours preparing and he never bothered to call you. Ask yourself, why, in the bigger scheme of things this is important to you? Let's break it down; was it inconsiderate and thoughtless of him? The answer is obvious but consider if this is a pattern or a one-time thing. If a pattern, you need to address your internal lack of self-respect because it appears you have drawn someone who simply does not respect your time. Let's go further; did you want to cook for him or were you doing it for some sort of agenda such as obligation or an alternative motive like needing validation or praise? And let's look at the spiritual overture. Was his being late some sort of divine intervention? Perhaps he avoided a car accident or needed to be in a certain place for a bigger purpose, those are the things many fail to consider when conflicts arise.

"How you argue is more important than what you are arguing about."

In every scenario of life which makes you angry or upset you, simply break it down and explore the reasons you are feeling what you are feeling. And always consider the spiritual overture, is there a bigger, greater reason which you can't see or do not have an explanation for? Ask yourself the tough questions and see all events as a cosmic mirror reflecting what in you, needs addressing. When you begin to see yourself honestly, your actions and the results of what you are putting out there, you will come to realize that everything is there to teach you and to heal you. You attract exactly what needs to be addressed from within; you attract exactly the scene which will benefit you the greatest as a catalyst to quantum leap your consciousness.

Let's explore how you fight with your spouse or with your mate,
Do you start by name calling or do you articulate?
Do you launch into a rant where nothing gets resolved?
Or do you stay calm and focused, the problem try to solve?

Do you bring up your mates past, throw in the kitchen sink?
Do you get resentful while your consciousness you shrink?
Arguing is normal but how you do it really says,
At what level's your intelligence, what's in your heart and head.

Staying calm in crisis allows Spirit to speak through,
Giving you solutions that getting angry robs from you.
It may not be about you but you make it personal,
Mates can just have a real bad day and upon you they hurl.

Speak with firm conviction but cooperate, seek to find,
A way to heal indifference, use both your heart and mind.
And don't forget to turn to God the power of prayer immense,
God is a great referee when times get too intense.

Today remember that disagreements are a normal part of humanness, however, there is an art to doing it effectively.

No two people on earth are exactly alike, so naturally we are not all going to agree on everything. How you argue and how you fight, is far more important than what you are actually fighting about. I was going to recite a few clinical studies on the effects of arguing but after reading reams of studies online, I discovered all of them were in direct conflict with each other! Even the comments were argumentative! You have got to love it when the professionals can't even agree on this topic. So in that vein, let me address the importance of how you argue and perhaps offer a spiritual perspective.

When you are fighting with your loved one, do you throw the kitchen sink in? Are you harboring old resentments which then rear their ugly head the minute a new fight arises? Do you hear what your partner is saying or in your mind are you dredging up previous battles to reinforce your case? It is human nature to become defensive but when you do, you eliminate the possibilities that anything will get resolved amicably.

"When you get defensive, you have already lost the battle."

One effective way to resolve conflict is to take a few deep breaths and remember who you are talking to. This is the person you love and every word is impacting your future relationship with that person, not to mention leaving a negative memory in their heart. Another critical ingredient is taking responsibility for your part in the scenario. No one is a victim. You have chosen it on some level to grow and learn from. Many will battle for the sake of winning, some just want to be right and others battle to jockey for position or power. Most don't realize until it is all said and done, that little has been gained from the fight. Watch how you speak to those you are intimate with, lovers, friends, partners and married couples. All souls have returned to intertwine and come together to resolve karma and resume where they left off previously. Many times our issues today are just a repeat from the past. You grow and change with every new lifetime so the dynamics change every time we reconnect. Many times as we are talking about someone, we don't realize that we are criticizing them or projecting our own unhealed issues. Watch those "digs", the little verbal barbs or bombs everyone has launched at someone they love in their lifetime. When you realize you are subtly projecting your anger and resentments on those in your life, you also will discover what you are harboring within. As we mature most of us learn innately to choose our battles wisely and mainly out of pure self-preservation, but when you break it down, in the final analysis, there is little worth fighting over.

Choose your battles wisely, evaluate the cost,
Is it worth your energy, what will be gained or lost?
What's the cost of spending your days in torrid rage?
Is it that important or best you turn the page?

Choose your battles wisely, don't argue and berate,
Execute diplomacy the hour is getting late.
Will you yet remember a year from now the fight?
Is it so important who is wrong or who is right?

Choose your battles wisely, don't give your pearls to those,
Who live inside inertia and will not be deposed.
Choose with wisdom and from heart, draw the battle line,
Move swiftly to solutions with all of humankind.

Choose your battles wisely, to this inference do lean,
You will feel the sting of words you said but didn't mean.
So take this day to recognize the price is much too high,
Think before you launch into a savage battle cry.

Choose your battles wisely. There is little on this planet which can be accomplished through fighting.

My ex-husband is still my closest friend and confidant so he doesn't mind me sharing a story with you. Years ago we were in Germany and were on our way to Strasbourg, France, which was about a two hour drive from his German hometown. His mom had triggered a few of his own issues that morning, so suffice to say he was not in a very good mood. As he drove, you could see him ruminating and churning inside, so the fight that ensued was of course, inevitable. He began yelling at decibel ranges which exceeded the sound of a freight train roaring through my head, and as I watched him flailing under the weight of his own internal damage, I tried to decide which method this time, would work to calm him down.

We were married for almost two decades, so by now I had become quite accustomed to these unexplained outbursts. For the first and last time, I decided to step out of character and try something different. My normal way was to let him unload and just be a good listener but this time I decided to try and match his tone, a technique I learned years earlier when conversing with clients. So even though I rarely, and I do mean rarely scream, I tried to scream at the same decibel range he was emoting at. Within just one short sentence, I burst into guttural laughter because this just wasn't that important to me and in fact I could not think of anything worth expending this kind of energy. I was not laughing at him of course, I was laughing at me, because it was so out of character for me and he was so shocked, that he actually stopped screaming immediately because he had never seen me scream!

Michael is a German and it is not their way to just segue from anger to laughter, so he became very quiet and within a half an hour we were in Strasbourg. As we got out of the car to go shopping and sightseeing, he reached over and as if nothing had ever happened, he gently took my hand and we strolled the city as if we were newlyweds. You see it wasn't about me.

"If this were your last day on earth, would you want to spend it on reaping discord?"

Many times there are wounds inside of the one you love and they are so deep, that they project the residual of that hurt onto you. That was certainly the case here and it takes patience and an open heart to really hear through the hurt, another is experiencing. In most arguments, it is rarely about what the fight started over, to begin with.

Many times we overlook what the core issues are. One of the reasons I teach and emphasize the importance of meditation in my sessions with clients, is that meditation opens up many new doors to inner healing and inner calm. When you stop emoting and center yourself, answers begin to surface. When you address your own pain, heartache, abandonment issues, mommy issues, resentment and fears, whatever you are feeling on the inside and projecting on the outside, your relationships improve.

"I am the total sum of my thoughts; every person in my life reflects my consciousness."

We are all just a reflection of each other. Let me rephrase that. We draw into our lives a mirrored reflection of what lies inside of us. It may include many dynamics and variables including karma, past or present, karma being the law of cause and effect, or may just be that you are drawing what you will best learn and grow from.

Arguments are a good catalyst to take a closer look at what you are harboring and what needs to be healed. Conflict is a normal part of humanness and can be healthy. Conflict teaches us to express ourselves, to be more diplomatic and tactful, to learn how to intertwine with others in our daily lives and to reconcile our own emotions. Conflict also teaches us how to be direct and honest with our feelings, how to be more specific in your own self-expression, leaving no ambiguity.

"Understanding and compassion are birthed from conflict."

"There are no greater answers than the ones that lie inside of you."

There is a way, taught by the masters and sages throughout the annals of time, to shift the paradigm in any situation. You see, life is a continuum where infinite possibilities and all that has ever been, runs like an eternal movie in the heavens. Some call it the Holograms, some call it the Book of Life, some call it the Akashic records. Others simply call it the variables of quantum physics. No matter what you name it, it is a moving, living, breathing constant and when you learn that you can step into the reality you dream of, the one you often sit and ponder or long for, when you implement and access the god within, you can shift your own personal paradigm. You simply close your eyes, see yourself already experiencing the joys of your perfect experience. See yourself step up and step into the fullness of your higher self, your god self, then hold the knowing that your vision is a reality and watch as it come into fruition. This exercise can be applied to something as simple as lowering your blood pressure or reducing your weight to even larger visions. It can even be applied to creating peace in the world. There is no limitation since the Collective Conscious holds every possible variable, every possible outcome; you get to choose it, from the lower dimensions to the highest will which is the most perfect scenario. Jesus said, "Know ye not that ye are gods?" He also said, "Everything I do can ye also do and more." You have the power and when wielded with love, there is no limitation to what you can be, have, or do.

> *"When answers can no longer be found outside, divine solutions unfold inside."*

First of all, steady yourself in the calm collective center of certainty, for life is meant to be focused on a path of flow, which is always available when you seek to tap into it. When you still your mind, the myriad expanse of divine love flows into you and higher light comes through, illumining the road ahead. The mountains do not move with force. They move with calm clarity and certainty. They move with love. Seek to see the road ahead as paved with your intentions and the flowers that line the path are the visible increments of the journey of realization, that all you dream is not only possible, it is inevitable. It all begins with the love you hold inside for yourself, for life, for your family, for your friends and the love you give and share with others. Love takes on many forms and comes in many ways. They can be love between families or the love you have for your children, the love you feel for your pets or being in love with a spouse or significant other. It can be love between friends and even the love you feel for those you have only met in social media. So many of us feel so connected and that kind of love is just as beautiful as any other kind of love.

But there is one kind of love that only a handful of people ever have the pure privilege of experiencing. The reasons are many, but the primary reason is that most are unaware of its' pure existence. Many have hardened themselves and cannot feel its' pure essence. It is that rare alignment of souls who have come together before in another lifetime. They find one another and heaven and earth moves in waves and beams to bring them together through DIVINE rhythms, through synchronized orchestration, no matter where they are in the world. And I am not just speaking of soul-mates and twin souls, I am talking about reconnecting with souls we have known before. They are those we shared a deep connection with or those we experienced profound events with. It happens every day when we meet someone we feel a connection with, yet most overlook how the universe conspired to bring you together with friends and family from the past. We are all interconnected, intertwined from many lifetimes together, returning to assist each other again or to heal past karma or just because we are of such a like vibration, that we are attracted to that profound and familiar force of energy.

"Love without an agenda encases energy so proportionate to God that it permeates the universe and leaves a mark on everything it touches."

On earth, love has many variances but in the universe there is only one "type" of love and it cannot be defined, for it is omnipresent. It is all encompassing and it transcends all fields of energy. It is love which has a strong foundation in something greater than the self, greater than satisfying the human cravings, greater than filling a space inside the wounds of your own heart. It is sacred beyond all measure, unconditional, complete and can stand alone and yet still feel connected. It is love which has no sunset and continues with every sunrise, love which does not complete you because in and of itself it is complete, whole, and perfect. When you align your heart to divine perfection, when you stand forth in your own perfection and surrender your soul to divine rhythms, to the highest will, what comes forth, what seeks to find you and will, is perfect love. You can choose to drink from the well of wisdom, power and love inside of you, or you can limit, even negate its flow, with your actions and inner dialogue. It is a choice but when you heal the heart and dissolve the ego, you rise to new heights, new wonders, and new worlds of delight. There is simply no limitation to what you can be, have or do for it is written, "I came that ye may have life and live it abundantly." *~Jesus*

Behold the Vision
A Walk in Wisdom

"Believe only that which your senses reveal for often the heart and mind are foe."

Every day we encounter a barrage of information from the internet to local, national and world news, to the thoughts and opinions of those we encounter on our journey and we make judgments on all of it. In our minds, we form our conceptions, misconceptions, values and belief systems and if we have opinionated friends or family, we are often influenced by what they believe, particularly when we are young and impressionable.

A considerable body of research conducted within the United States, has overwhelmingly demonstrated the profound influence of parents' beliefs and behaviors on children's educational aspirations and academic achievement. As we grow older and go through our own personal evolution, we form even more beliefs, often as an emotional response to our environment or events in our lives, which mold our perceptions and often set them in stone.

In my practice I often discover, much to my chagrin, that my clients have preconceived notions about meditation, even though many have never meditated. Some people show aversion to certain healing modalities because of what they've "heard." I recently encountered a guy in social media who is a certified life coach and spiritual psychologist who reached out to me for help. At the end of the conversation I was shocked when he rejected the idea of praying together for resolve, to seal his intentions and to put them into motion. His fear of praying with someone he didn't know, well over-rode his common sense. It also revealed his own self-sabotage in action.

There is overwhelming evidence that many people in America have become overly dependent on prescription drugs because they were taught to take a pill for every ache and pain they encounter. Every day we form new preconceived notions and beliefs. Some are fed from ignorance or a lack of information, some fed from fear or hate and some are fed from a lack of education or socio-economic conditioning. Others simply come from imagination, ego, or dysfunction.

I had a client many years ago who was the son of one of the wealthiest men in the world. His father was and is a staple on the Forbes richest men in America list. One Sunday, this young man stumbled into one of my lectures at The Rainbow Ray Focus Church. Both father and son were Jewish but David had broken away from his beliefs as many young people do, to explore the lives of masters from other cultures, one of those being Jesus. As I mentioned beforehand, when I died in 1993 in the Alps of Austria I had a very personal encounter with Jesus, Buddha and many others waiting in the Light. When David's' father heard that he was taking my courses, he could not board a plane fast enough. When we met, it was no surprise to me that we loved each other instantly.

That evening, we dined together at a quaint little restaurant in Sedona, Arizona known for its unique ambiance and cuisine. As Michael, David's father, queried me about what I was teaching his son, he began to share his beliefs about Jesus which, to say the least, I had heard before from some of my other Jewish friends. I shared that a part of my death experience was learning to honor all other cultures and religions, but subscribe to none, save love, or I would miss the boat on teaching those who really needed it the most.

I was raised in a traditional Baptist family, going to church every Sunday and Wednesday, and attending vacation Bible school during the summer. But it was not until I died, that I found out how much more I had lived, not just in this lifetime, but in many others, things they did not teach me in Bible school. I was shown by Jesus in such a way, that there was simply no disputing reincarnation or the reality of previous lives.

Well, needless to say, sharing all this with a devoutly Jewish man was a bit intimidating but I continued to share anyway. Taking people outside of their comfort zone is one of my best tools for teaching.

By the end of dinner, I surprisingly found myself ready to convert to Judaism! David's father was just as passionate about his own beliefs and was very convicted and convincing. He has spent his whole life denying the existence of Jesus, without even acknowledging his good works. It's one thing to be skeptical, but it's an entirely different thing to denounce. I was not arrogant enough to believe that I needed to defend Jesus' honor nor was I here to convince anyone of his role on this earth. But this opportunity presented a great catalyst to elaborate on the bigger picture. I suddenly and deliberately leaned over very close to David's dad. In a very quiet but distinct tone I asked a very simple but thought provoking question, "What if you are wrong? What if you have lived your entire life locked down to a belief that negates the contributions of a pinnacle figure to millions? What if you have lived a lie which degredated and completely negated the life work of an extraordinary human being?" His answer surprised me and gave me chills. With a dumbfounded look on his face he simply replied, "Ariaa that never occurred to me."

You see, many times we do just that. We live our life locked into a way of thinking that prevents us from experiencing life in extraordinary ways and from connecting even more to our higher aspects where angels can be seen and heard. To allow your mind to become fixed on one way of thinking is to enable death, the death of ideas, open mindedness, and essentially your own growth.

Did you know that what you think and what you fix in mind
Can generate the death of growth and limit the Divine?
When you fail to look at all the views in the debate
You seal yourself from knowledge and that staunchness seals your fate.

As we age we all become so set in all our ways
We think we know it all and yet most live inside a haze.
If you think you know it all then your life should really flow
Everything so perfect in all you reap and sow.

If you know it all, then why the pain and why the tears?
If you know it all, then why the doubt and all those fears?
If you know it all, then why do you keep seeking so?
If you know it all, then God should heal you, you'd be whole.

If you know it all, then why aren't your gifts increased?
If you know it all, then why's your ego so unleashed?
If you know it all, then why aren't angels tapping you?
To heal the sick and raise the dead and feed the masses too?

You see that no one knows it all, no matter what you read
Reading books does not improve your faith or your belief.
Defensiveness reveals a lot and volumes does it speak
Open up and listen for humble pie will make you meek.

"And the meek shall inherit the earth" *Matthew. 5:5*

It's easy to get locked in to one way of thinking but things aren't always what they seem. It reminds me of the story of the two traveling angels whose author remains unknown but it is such a great reminder about perspective.

"Two traveling angels stopped to spend the night in the home of a wealthy family. The family was rude and refused to let the angels stay in the mansion's guest room. Instead the angels were given a small space in the cold basement. As they made their bed on the hard floor, the older angel saw a hole in the wall and repaired it. When the younger angel asked why, the older angel replied, "Things aren't always what they seem.""

"The next night the pair came to rest at the house of a very poor, but very hospitable farmer and his wife. After sharing what little food they had, the couple let the angels sleep in their bed where they could have a good night's rest."

"When the sun came up the next morning, the angels found the farmer and his wife in tears. Their only cow, whose milk had been their sole income, lay dead in the field."

"The younger angel was infuriated and asked the older angel, "How could you have let this happen?"

"The first man had everything, yet you helped him", she accused.

"The second family had little but was willing to share

everything, and you let the cow die!"

"Things aren't always what they seem," the older angel replied."

"When we stayed in the basement of the mansion, I noticed there was gold stored in that hole in the wall. Since the owner was so obsessed with greed and unwilling to share his good fortune, I sealed the wall so he wouldn't find it."

"Then last night as we slept in the farmer's bed, the angel of death came for his wife. I gave him the cow instead. So you see, things aren't always what they seem."

"Reach beyond the veils which blind you from the light for the greatest fruits lay beyond the branches."

Many of you remember when Oprah Winfrey and Gayle King took a road trip together landing in Arizona at one of the Indian reservations. Reading directly from Oprah's site, this is what they found as they entered:

"On the morning of day three, Oprah and Gayle set out toward Window Rock, Arizona, the capital and spiritual heart of Navajo nation. The area around Window Rock is home to more than 270,000 Navajo people. In the 1860s, more than 10,000 Navajo were forced from their land and marched to a desolate reservation 450 miles away. The "long walk" is a painful legacy still felt today in places like Window Rock, where unemployment is a staggering 43 percent and almost 56 percent of people live below the poverty line. While some Navajo do not have the resources to leave this poverty-stricken area, others refuse to abandon the sacred land of their ancestors." Here, a belief system no matter how sacred, is keeping these people from living a better life with running water and sewage but they choose to stay. It always comes down to a choice.

"The universe does not judge you for what you choose. They only assist you in getting it."

Since earth is a free will zone, your guides and angels do not judge what you have chosen nor do they try to influence you unless you actually ask for guidance on what you are seeking to understand or know. Angels and the universe simply do not decipher. You choose what you give allegiance to, what you wish to believe and what you set in your mind as your own truth. You do this in more ways than you realize, through books, television, movies, social media, family, friends, religions, traditions and socio-economic circumstances. Some blaze a trail with their own ideas and other succumb to what has been passed on to them from these avenues.

I encountered a man at a store who parked at the same time I did. In the back of his very small truck he had two huge dogs. They were rambunctious and you could just see them falling out of that truck while playing with each other. I tried to gently mention how concerned I was for the safety of his pets. His response was one of arrogance and ignorance. He said snidely laughing, "Welcome to America where I can do what I want!"

I just shook my head and kept walking, realizing that his belief had nothing to do with the well-being of the animals or even common sense. His belief was that, as an American, he could do whatever he wanted and damn the consequences. Sadly, his beliefs could cause harm to innocent animals, but it is the same with humans. Many people make major decisions without considering the consequences of their choices and without considering the impact their choices may have on those around them. Society has adopted a "me-me-me" attitude more over the past several decades to the detriment of humankind.

What a shame that some still believe in the antiquated need to kill each other or engage in war. What a shame that that some people believe homosexuality is bad or that you can get AIDS from simply being around an HIV positive person. What a shame that our society is now engaged in diluting the gene pool by viewing reality shows which capitalize on the crude or gross, with higher ratings for featuring ignorance and the height of bad behavior. Are we Neanderthals, unable to coexist in harmony and peace with all the advantages of education, spiritual wisdom and the ability to communicate, greater than at any other time on earth?

I urge you to ask yourself in every scenario,

What if I am WRONG?

What if you ARE wrong?

What if you can be FREE of cancer or any other disease?

What if gay people are PERFECT and marriage is not only a human right but a DIVINE RIGHT for all consenting adults?

What if PEACE is the ONLY way?

What if animals are ANGELS in disguise?

What if you can HEAL yourself from sickness or poverty?

What if you can be free from DEBT, free from SUFFERING, free from GUILT, free from any BELIEFS that limit your ability to be HAPPY?

What if?

No one is a victim. Not one soul on this earth is subject to anything. Whether you acknowledge it or not there is but one ultimate truth, we choose it all! I know this is a very hard concept to wrap your brain around but lend an ear anyway. When you see those you perceive as a victim, consider that what you are not seeing is the total picture of what they have done in other lifetimes, who they have done it to and what they have come to earth to learn or repay. On some level, we choose it all including how much energy we pour into what we believe. It is time we all take personal responsibility for what we are projecting onto other people, other cultures, other nations and each other. It is high time everyone begin to ask, "What if, I AM WRONG?" What if I have lived an entire life committed to a falsehood, or perpetuating my beliefs on others causing pain or heartache to another or causing them to feel as if they are less? What if I have lived my life persecuting someone because they did not agree with something I believed? What if I'm WRONG?

Imagine and would you just allow your mind to take this trip…
What you could be on any day with God's workmanship?
You have the mind to heal your soul, a soul to heal your mind
You have a body wondrous, illumined with great light.

You have an information wheel, a brain which can define
What comes from love, what comes from light, and what needs most aligned.
You have the power to go within and heal your fears and doubts
You choose to drink from God's great well or choose to live in drought.

Imagine freeing yourself from the harboring of pain
Imagine being free from old beliefs which are ingrained.
Free yourself and just forgive all souls with full embrace
Be the brighter light of God and extend the greater grace.

Imagine if you saw yourself of love, complete and whole
Imagine that transforming light which causes you to grow.
You have that love, you own that light, you are complete I say,
Choose to be a healthy, happy person every day. It is a choice.

"Your attitude is paramount to shifting your circumstances and every thought you think generates a response." *Ariaa Jaeger, "The Book of Ariaa"*

"By choosing your thoughts, and by selecting which emotional currents you will release and which you will reinforce, you determine the quality of your Light. You determine the effects that you will have upon others, and the nature of the experiences of your life." *Gary Zukav, "Seat Of the Soul"*

"If we understood the power of our thoughts, we would guard them more closely.

If we understood the awesome power of our words, we would prefer silence to almost anything negative. In our thoughts and words we create our own weaknesses and our own strengths. Our limitations and joys begin in our hearts. We can always replace negative with positive." *Bettie Eadie, "Embraced By the Light"*

"It has been said that man can create anything which he can imagine." *Napoleon Hill, "Think and Grow Rich"*

We create in many ways, some conscious, others subconscious and some from a spiritual level of consciousness. Often we are not in sync with what we came to this earth to sow, to learn from or to contribute to. But there is a divine cord which keeps us near the path we, as souls, first set our sights upon. While many times we may find ourselves wandering away from that higher plan, it is rare we that don't find our way back to it.

Manifestations begin with a single thought, the spark of energy that lights the flame of continuation. It spins and spirals into the universe where angels receive their charge and light the flame to quicken its flow. Your intensity, your passion and desire then propel it further into the maze where all thoughts go, known as the collective conscience. It searches then encircles your previous thoughts aligned to the same frequency, then like a boomerang it returns to you with the same amount of energy you poured into creating it. Whether you intended it or not, if you think it in some way or fashion, it is so.

How do you know if you are off the path? It's simple, consequences. Those are the events, good, bad, or indifferent, which take place when you have chosen a lower path. That is not to say it is punishment as the Universe was created from love and the earth was created with free will. You are free to experience whatever you want, whatever you need to learn, or however you will best achieve whatever your intended life lessons are. Every soul functions at a different level of consciousness, therefore we all learn differently. However, the laws of attraction are clear, whatever you resist persists.

"What you LOVE, you MAGNIFY

What you HATE, you DRAW

What you FEAR, you AMPLIFY

What you ENERGIZE, you ATTRACT

Over the past several decades, society as a whole has evolved both intellectually and spiritually, resulting in millions of people awakening and becoming keenly aware that thoughts are things. In the early 1950's, the great Norman Vincent Peale penned a top bestseller entitled "The Power of Positive Thinking" which was considered revolutionary. "The Secret" and other similar books on the laws of attraction have once again, raised the awareness that we are magnets, walking this planet, attracting what we are thinking and that is absolute truth. Everyone, with rare exception, knows that you attract into your life a reflection of what you think. But you also attract into your life what you judge. If you think men are players, you attract players. If you think people are dishonest, you attract dishonest people. If you are focused on a sickness or disease, you attract exactly that. If you focus on poverty or lack, you gain nothing more than an empty bank account.

"Holding the vision brings forth the means."

Everything you hold in your conscious thought either becomes your cage or your wings and creates your ultimate reality. Each day, own your thoughts, own your truth, and own the reality you are creating with every unhealed fear or with every unattended thought. Conversely, you can really create at rapid speed using positive affirmations and deliberate thinking. It is by your intention that you are known in heavenly realms. The angels and your guides can see how much intention you are pouring into anything, the greater the energy and passion, the quicker the magnified return.

Why not fake until you make it folks.

See abundance.

See honesty in all.

Embrace good, healthy, emotionally healthy people.

Focus on the beauty and not the ugly.

And fix what hurts you, heal what aches, mend your mind and restore it to perfection.

You were born of perfection.

It is your core.

Meditate, exercise, eat nutritionally, and address what you are harboring.

Only then, will you attract lovely all day long.

When you add the additional ingredient, 'knowing" into the equation, your thoughts really become more expansive. There are four laws of Creation. The first is the idea or concept. The second law of creation is the spoken word. The third law of Creation is gratitude, giving thanks as if it is already accomplished. The final, fourth law of Creation is the vital element, knowing. You have to know that you know that you know. If one glint of doubt enters into your thoughts, it burrows a hole into the entire creation. The key is to ward off those thoughts which kill or nullify what you are trying to create. You do this by constantly bombarding your own thoughts with positive ones. You are in control of all of it and random thoughts will produce, too.

There is one other element which few recognize but it is a master level teaching that says, if you want to create anything, do not speak about it. Hold it in your thoughts, prayers and visions and allow the energy of the desire to amass. When you tell everyone about it, you actually punch holes in the energy where it scatters and dissipates. Holding it in your consciousness while holding the vision will actually accelerate its creation.

*"The Universe revolves and evolves
through synchronistic knowing."*

I wake up with the sunrise and every day I know
A warm sun will awaken me with its all impressive glow.
I rise to greet the morning and my eyes behold the love
Of my pets who just like children, are a gift from up above.

I know the water will flow to bathe me till I glow
There's food to fill my body for energy to go.
I know I'll bask in light supreme when with God I commune
I know Archangels are with me in this very room.

The knowing is a state of mind, you can embrace it too
The knowing is a state of grace which always follows you.
The knowing is a faith divine, those mountains will be moved
The knowing is for one like me a form of godly food.

Start with knowing that your life is in God's highest will
Embrace that you have purpose here and it will be fulfilled.
Know you're loved, you're healthy, whole and know your needs are met
Know you're living as you should, there's nothing to regret.

Know your dreams are realized and know there's more to come
Know the darkness passes by, know not to come undone.
Know you're where you're supposed to be on any given day
Know you have the chance to change life every time you pray.

> *"Your inner dialogue either raises your spiritual frequency or it lowers it."*

I would like to expound upon that theme a little more by addressing your verbiage and how you are applying language in your everyday life. Words carry amassed energy from thousands of year's usage. If you look at words like "love" and 'hate' and how they have been used throughout the millennial, you'll begin to understand why some thoughts create faster than others. Words have power, but your intentions are the energy that brings the words to life, your intent is the fuel.

How much energy are you pouring into "catching" the flu? I hear many of you actually tell me that you are catching a cold! How much energy do you pour into "being broke" or running to the doctor to constantly search and be tested for diseases you will probably never get, unless you keep looking for them, that is. The mind is a very potent machine capable of creating anything and imprinting everything.

> *"Speak it, and by the conviction of your own words, will it be done."*

I'm reminded of the late actor, Christopher Reeve who played "Superman." Six months before his horseback riding accident which ended in lifetime paralysis, he played the part of a paraplegic police officer in HBO's, "Above Suspicion." To prepare for the role, he said that he would lie in bed at night with sand bags on his legs, so he could really experience what it felt like to be paralyzed from the waist down.

Farrah Fawcett said that she virtually got lost in her role as a battered wife in the "Burning Bed" and then was beaten severely by her estranged boyfriend moviemaker James Orr, who was later convicted of the charge.

The hilarious comedian Jim Carrey used his mind to create something quite wonderful. Jim was taking odd jobs and occasionally performing at low end night clubs when in 1983, he wrote himself a check in the amount of 10 million dollars and postdated it for 10 years from that day. He noted, "For acting services rendered." He folded it up and put it in his wallet and every night after work he would drive up to Mulholland Drive, get out of the car, take the check out of his wallet and hold it up to the sky to show to the universe. He then opened his arms, closed his eyes and envisioned dollar bills falling from the heavens into his hands. He said he did this night after night for quite some time. In 1993, on the very day the check was dated for, he signed a deal to star in "The Mask" for 10 million dollars for "acting services rendered."

Listen and I'll tell you, for there is no greater truth
If you say to the mountain go, then the mountain shall be moved.

Your words are moving energy, propelled by your intent
What you say will multiply whether or not you consent.

Whether you intended it, makes no difference here
The law of the invisible is written and it's clear.

The words you speak may have no power but your intentions do
If it springs forth from your lips, it's already done to you.

When words are used maliciously or for verbal attack
Those words will multiply in form and boomerang right back.

Each word you utter can create, at high levels if you trust
With faith and love dreams can come true but knowing is a must.

When words are used to send out love without intent to gain
What you do for others will be done to you in same.

However much you poured your heart into what you say
Will determine what comes back to you, times ten times ten today.

"Be aware of how you are using language and engage in a dialogue which uplifts."

As human beings we often forget the amount of power we can generate with a simple thought. In my own spiritual evolution I have reached a level of consciousness where I have to stay on top of my thoughts and ensure they are positive or they create at light-speed instantly! I will give you an example. Using a video editing software program I recently tried to upload a picture from my computer to write one of my Ariaa Quotes. I have created hundreds over the last few years so I am very familiar with the software program. I was scouring through thousands of photos I have in my picture folder and found a beautiful, albeit provocative, picture, I wanted to use for a quote about intuition. I stared at that picture for perhaps thirty seconds and really wanted to use it, but thought it too early in the morning for such a picture and was concerned some of my social media followers would be offended. So I scrolled down about four or five rows and found a very sanitized picture I could use and as I clicked on it to upload it, the other provocative picture uploaded! I knew instantly that my intention was read and received by the universe, thus the picture loaded itself. Your higher self is always at work whether you know it or not and even though most override their higher good from fears, beliefs or other lower emotions, many times the highest comes forth anyway. Needless to say, I used the provocative picture to illustrate my quote.

> *"Unlock the doors to your mind*
> *and the possibilities are endless."*

Did you know that thoughts are things which manifest in kind?
Did you know you only use just one tenth of your mind?
Imagine now what you could do if you would take heed…
To these words which will affect the way your thoughts succeed.

God made man in his image and love commands the fold
When you think and speak with love, a new world you'll behold.
Positive in all you say will quicken what comes forth
The more you do this every day the more you'll know it's worth.

Start each day with prayerful words giving love and praise
Give thanks and have a grateful heart as the sun beams forth its rays.
As you shower or drive to work create the day you choose
Happy, healthy, prosperous, with those thoughts you can't lose.

Write it in a journal, the dreams you dream in words
Make some affirmations your future you'll secure.
Formulate your thoughts each day and get attuned to light
There are no limitations, your thoughts will take to flight.

The Universe helps those who help themselves and everything you put into the universe returns in one form or another. Most people know about the laws of attraction but there are other variables which determine the magnitude of what returns. Some may only experience a mild return while others get slammed from their thoughts and actions. The more spiritually awake you are, the quicker the return. The more you know, the more you summon the universe and its cooperation with your spirit. Your spirit is always trying to find its way back to the Source or Creator. The closer to the core you get, the more pronounced your psychic and spiritual activity become. It may feel a little unfair at times since so many who are unawake, seem to never get their negative karma back, like those who hurt others. Everyone without exception is subject to the return of karma and the longer it takes, the more powerful it becomes. If you "avoid" the return of karma by choosing a new sublime lifetime where everything is blissful, or you prolong the return of negative karma, it multiplies. That is one of the reasons some people seem to have such awful lives. They have either amassed a great deal of negative return or they have avoided repaying it in several lifetimes.

When you leave this earth, angels and your guides await you at Shamballa, the hall of lights and you have the opportunity to review the Akashic records, otherwise known as the Lamb's Book of Life. The Akashic records are a moving hologram, a life continuum, where all thoughts, actions and everything in the universe are recorded. Since there is no marker for time on the other side, there isn't any calendar date of events. It is as if all is still occurring present day time. You literally watch yourself from the 1800's, the 1500's, Biblical times, or any other lifetimes you have lived. Most human beings have an average of between 80-200 lifetimes, though that can vary, depending on the mastery of the soul. The number of lifetimes does not necessarily connote mastery or an evolved soul. Some people who have fewer lifetimes but who learn at an accelerated rate are often more evolved than those who have many more lifetimes. The angels' help you assess what you accomplished, what karma you amassed, both positive and negative, and they help you decide what to choose for your next incarnation. You choose your family, your circumstances, such as being born rich or poor, you choose the country or ethnicity you wish to be born in and you decide approximately how long earth time it is going to take you to accomplish all of it. Then you get to planet earth and forget everything, the universal cosmic joke. People often ask me why we don't remember every lifetime with all the details and that is simple to answer. Most people don't remember because they would come back and want to reclaim their castle, car, land or mates and would linger in the past, thus never truly evolving, and the entire purpose to come to earth is to grow.

Deep in your heart, you have mastered so many areas of consciousness in other incarnations. In previous lifetimes, most people have chosen to be a variety of different races and have played roles such as monks, priests, nuns, warriors, royalty, pauper, martyr and even saint. And in each existence you choose the circumstance of your life. Many will ask, "Why would I choose to get Bubonic plague or to be beheaded?" The answer is that trauma and drama are a great catalyst for evolution. Many fail to see that being poor, or being blind or being falsely accused are actually blessings in disguise.

*"Today remember that doubt scatters faith
and dissolves seeds of knowing."*

I walked the halls of darkness, of sorrow, hardship, and pain,
I hungered for a time, and was soaked by drenching rain.

I gathered light and energy as I rose up every time,
I fought with self but mastered the soul's great redesign.

With every challenge, there were seeds of wisdom planted deep,
With every woe I learned to rise, to dance, to sow, to reap.

The blessings in the hardship at times I could not see,
But o'er they came in waves and beams and so enveloped me.

I heard a wise man say once, "Great souls endure great trials",
But one must open their heart and mind to navigate the aisles.

It's wise to learn to celebrate the daunting ways of life,
For what you can't behold on earth is written in the skies.

You gain your greatness not from ease but from the maddening page,
Your light grows greater with each turn, as you become…

The Sage

I sought love but love eluded me,

I sought peace and wars broke out,

I sought loyalty and friends betrayed me,

I sought refuge and my home was taken away.

I sought to add wisdom but they would not listen,

I sought to heal the world but the world became undone,

I sought to soothe the masses but the cries of the mad were deafening.

I sought to raise the consciousness and only raised my own.

Then I saw a realm paradisiacal and beheld the ultimate epiphany.

I sought love and found I was its' instrument, it lives and breathes in me.

I sought peace and found I was its beacon, it emanated from my own inner peace.

I sought loyalty and discovered that the purest loyalty is being true to myself.

ought refuge and found that nature and heaven were my home.

I sought to add wisdom and discovered it thrives in all living creation but they must be willing to hear.

I sought to heal the world and found it was perfect in all its self-destruction and that at the core of all the chaos, lives all that is divine.

I sought to soothe the masses yet found it is in the cries of the maddening crowd that the darkness is exposed and transformed by the greater light of God.

I sought to raise the consciousness and found that in raising my own, my eyes beheld the ONE.

You make the life you want through the implementation of both the negatives and positives. Do you give life to worry, fear, abandonment, sickness or hopelessness, or do you birth wonder, love, joy and infinite possibilities? You are the parent to your thoughts, you can either discipline them or let them run amuck and control you. You can raise them up to create new worlds or you can let them mow you down and create chaos. It is a choice. What kind of parent are you to thought, what kind of mentor are you to YOU? Inspire yourself, be kind to your heart, be good to your body, let love and all things loving fill you and you will bring to life miracles and blessings.

Rise with me in shades of light that permeate the new,
Behold horizons unexplored with joyful overview.
Expand your walk by giving of your heart and soul,
Live your life on purpose and a new world will unfold.

The Shadows Edge

"Be aware of the shadow you cast upon humankind; does it bring shade or does it prevent light?"

Shadows are the imprint of past life traumas and everyone without exception has them. If you are spiritually unawake, your own shadows will convince you that you are being attacked by an outer entity or force. Demons, on the other hand, are outside forces which are there to prevent you from your higher infusion of divine light. They attack only when you are at your lowest point emotionally. In every spiritual seeker's life, you will encounter both along the road of evolution but they are not to be feared. In fact, it is the contrary as both are beneficiary to going higher. The higher you go, the more you will draw them to your soul. The universe is created with opposite polarities. Without dark you would not know light, without light, you would not know darkness. Most souls have worked with both the higher worlds and the lower worlds in previous incarnations. Let's say you were a great warrior and you killed others in battle for a kingdom and let's say you were really good at it. The lower worlds would like to keep you since you did such a good job for their team so they would prefer you live in limitation. Their role is to keep people suffering, miserable, impoverished and full of fears. Now let's say you also had lifetimes where you did wonderful things in the name of God or the light in many lifetimes. Naturally the higher worlds would love to see you continue the good works but they also do not have an agenda since earth is a free will zone and there simply is no judgment to what you choose.

You can easily detect your own shadows by watching your reactions to events and circumstances or in those moments of complacency when you should act, but don't. One of my biggest pet peeves with human beings is their complacency when they see something unjust occurring. This has become particularly acute in social media where many people continue to follow haters, bullies and drama makers, simply because they fear becoming their target or they just don't have a strong character and the courage to stand up for injustice. Perhaps it is their own unhealed past life shadows which are veiling their ability to have courage or to be forthright and wise. It is one of the critical reasons why I encourage my clients to tackle and embrace their shadows because being weak-willed and having little to no character is not the way human beings were originally designed. Goodness lives at the core of all human beings, but actuating it is an entirely individual thing.

Do you see a pattern of repetition in your own personality which lends itself to a shadow? Do you do the same things over and over again and have behaviors which are unsavory and habitual? Do you act out, never questioning how it is going to impact the receiver of your actions? Do you stop to think about the pain your actions may cause another who has no idea of your own unhealed issues? Do you ever stop to look at why you do the things you do, why you act the way you do, why you say the things you say? Are you functioning from a healthy place or from dysfunction? Do you do things just to get attention because you lack self-love? Do you put on a dog and pony show pretending to have it all together when your life is nothing more than a pretense of what you wish you really were? Then look inside and ask the question, "Why?" If you have not assessed yourself and taken a hard look at those elements which stem from emotional bleeding, then you are missing the very reason you are on planet earth.

When you are really honest with yourself, when you really open your heart to understanding yourself, you can then identify what needs healing, modifying, or perfecting. If everyone would work on their own internal well-being and stop pointing the finger at politicians, the government, friends, and enemies, those you think hurt you, those you hurt; if everyone would take personal responsibility for what each are creating, the world would change dramatically. If everyone would spend as much time on fixing what is wrong inside of them instead of blaming others for their lot, even the universal collective conscious would change. Be an active participant by asking yourself that all important question, "WHY am I behaving like this?"

Sadly, many have become hardened or jaded by life and hide their essential self for fear of being too vulnerable and taken advantage of. If you listen, you will hear people express opinions that are jaded from the road of hardship. Society has become desensitized from watching reality shows where people hurt each other, beat each other up or throw verbal assaults. We often craft our opinions from our pain, hurts and slights. The sweetness and innocence within, often becomes buried under the siege of life's mortar. It is time to soften your sinews, to evaluate what you are saying, to heal what is hurting you, and to address those shadows which veil you from living a luminous life. For the vibration of love to thrive, the vibration of humanity must be healthy. For humanity to be physically healthy, humans must be emotionally healthy first. Sickness and dis-ease are a byproduct of emotional unhappiness.

"A victim mentality negates a victorious outcome."

"You did this to me"; "No, you did that to me"; "Well, they did this to me"; "My mother did that to me"; "My father is to blame"; "It's the governments fault"; "It's God punishing me"...

That is the dialogue of the unawakened spiritual traveler who goes through life as a victim. It's everyone else's fault; no job, poor health, no education, no friends, no peace? When you point the finger, you give your power away to everyone you are blaming for your choices and the circumstances you came to this earth to master. You created all of it and if you doubt that, you doubt God, Jesus, Buddha and countless other sages who have all said the same thing. The kingdom lies within you, you are god and one with God and so is everyone else.

"No one can do anything to you unless you allow it."

When you or those you know act out and point a blaming finger for all they think "you" have done to them, remember this simple spiritual principle. We are all cosmic mirrors to one another, reflecting what needs healing in each other. The mirror reflects in both directions, to you and the one you are battling, with rare exception but there is one very important exception.

There are a handful of souls on the planet, who are on the path to reaching full enlightenment. For them, the road is more challenging since many they encounter are not reflections of something internal, but rather are catalysts to catapult to another level. That being said, the majority of people will attract a mirrored reflection of what dwells within them.

In all circumstances, evaluate what you added to the debate or dialogue and be truthful with yourself. Then you will heal what needs to be healed. Take yourself to task and ask "Why did I draw this to me? What am I trying to learn from it and what are the higher solutions that will bring forth the greatest healing for me?" When you take personal responsibility for your own emotional issues, the mirror becomes a gift and shines a divine light on that which is eager for you to embrace and integrate. You are a reflection to all and everything and everyone is a reflection of you.

Every answer you will ever need, resides within you, but you have to be willing to hear them. You have to silence the ego and hear with the heart. When you fail to take responsibility for your actions and what thoughts you project onto others and into the world, you lower your own vibration. That lessens the chance of finding the higher solutions. When you address and own your baggage, your mommy damage, your daddy damage, your actions, your judgments, your misconceptions, your fears, shadows and dark side, you add higher light, illuminating the road ahead. In doing so you strip away the veils where the highest paradigm or highest will can be accessed and that ensures the greatest flow in your life.

"Be aware that you are the living experience of the laws of cause and effect"

Own your life and all you are attracting. The consequences you are experiencing are of your own creation and can teach you greatly when you embrace the total sum of all you are and what you are doing, to attract everything you are experiencing. I know life can be painful as I have experienced things in my own life that have left me riddled with scars. Yet I learned early on, that those scars do heal if you welcome change and move through the process with expeditious grace. By embracing the lessons and extracting the benefits of your circumstances, you evolve, then, what was once your heartache is suddenly transformed into the wisdom that lines the path of knowing.

Karma often plays a big role in what you are attracting and staying immersed in the hardship of the circumstance, supports the lingering of karma. When you own it, review it, integrate it and heal it, you move through the karma rapidly and help dissolve it. Once it is behind you, if you maintain a dialogue of kindness and behave according to the laws of love, you will not have to experience it again.

There are people on this earth who cause other people pain
There are souls who just by living life can bring forth storms and rain.
Then there are the souls who live to uplift and inspire
There are those who love with all their heart and with all of their fire.

What do you cause as you wander through this world of light?
What do you leave in the way of dramas, baggage, strife?
Do you leave a mark of love on everything you touch?
What do you give of yourself or withhold and fiercely clutch?

Do you whine and cry about that which you cannot change?
Do you live inside the past or with vision broaden range?
Do you see your future and the potential of your state?
Souls are much more beautiful when dining from God's plate.

The effect you cause on other's lives is lasting, please take heed
Learn to be consistent, tune to other peoples' needs.
Though you cannot be all things to everyone you know
You can be the spark which lights the flame, the nurtured seed that grows.

Everyone has an egg, some people wear them on the inside and some people wear them on the outside. Whether wounds, hurts, slights, resentments or fears from childhood which bleed through in their behavior today, whether abandonment, fear of success, fear of commitment, fear of the unknown, betrayal or betraying, insecurity, lack of self-worth, self-love, lack of character or integrity, no matter what the cause, everyone has an egg. The goal is to look beyond the obvious, straight into the heart of every person. When you see others with your heart, through the eyes of love and perfection, when you behold all people as they were created, perfect and pure at the core, you actually raise their vibration and perfection by beholding them in that light.

> *"People respond to you in exactly the same way as you feel about yourself."*

See not the flaws in humans but instead see the beauty in every soul. Listen to those around you with an open heart. If you really tune in you will see beyond their words, straight into their heart. See not your expectations of what you want them to be or how you want them to change, feel or even behave. Open your heart and see what they already are at the very core of their being. All are gods with incomprehensible power inside and all are comprised of the very breath of perfection. Every human being is perfect in spirit, yet all are learning how to crack the emotional egg, to feast on the pure food of the soul, love. Everyone without exception is working on some unsavory trait, habit, emotional pain, physical ailment or just plain spiritually evolving. But be clear that at the core of all beings lives pure perfection and uncovering the veils of life runs akin to peeling an onion. The more layers of skin you remove the more you get to the foundation of the onion. The more layers of shadows you remove from a human soul and the more you unearth their cellular memories, the more you get to the foundation of that soul and that foundation is quantum love.

"Be true to yourself and who you are, don't let the actions of anyone define you."

Are you listening to the voice of dysfunction? You know those messages and labels from childhood others cast upon you which have never truly faded? Are you hearing the clamor of ignorance from those who were raised at a time when humans were not the most psychologically evolved and did not have a clue how their actions and words could sear scars into the hearts of innocence? We have all had folks from our past say unkind things, even if well-intentioned and those tape recorded messages seared into the soul, re-run in our heads, when you least expect it.

But you are an adult now, capable of defining yourself and you can choose to hear the rhetoric of the past or you can choose to embrace yourself and define your own truth. Just because a parent, a sibling, or a total stranger said it of you, does not necessarily make it so. No one defines you, but you. When you go to bed at night, assess what you did today, how you could have done it differently to achieve a better outcome? When you are honest with yourself, when you give your best each day, most will claim the inner peace that comes with knowing you gave life the best of you.

Actions, words and deeds define you, not the opinions of others and not the opinions of those you love. You and only you can create or destroy your self-image, your self-worth, your self-love and your self-confidence. Stop blaming your parents, your siblings and the bullies in your life and make a conscious decision to define yourself! If you fail to define yourself, then do not be surprised if others do it for you.

"What are you creating with your behavior every day?

What are you empowering in the things you think and say?

What do you put in the world which boomerangs right back?

Do you feel the victim to your own karmic attack?

Do you blame the world around for what comes back to you?

Or do you see your thoughts and words just multiplied and grew?

The way you treat those in your life,

The things you say and think

Will be the measure of your life, the well from which you drink."

The Rabid Seed

"The lower worlds of demonics are real and your actions, thought and deeds either enable them or deflect them."

Demons are an earthly reality and they come when you least expect them and usually it is when you are sick or depressed, under a lot of pressure or weak from being emotionally wrought. You see stories of mass killings in the news every day which profile people who were thought to be balanced, healthy and productive, and then they suddenly kill for no apparent reason. Many times it is demons, entities, those dark, shadowy figures spoken of in every ancient book from the beginning to time. The reason they are so predominant these days, speaks volumes to the times in which we are living and one of the main reasons there are so many people struggling with demons, is fear. Fear feeds them, anger feeds them, and hate feeds demons, too. When you realize how much the darkness enjoys "undoing" you and that you are giving your power up every time you fear them, you will learn how to deal with them more effectively.

Those of you who have an aversion to religions may not want to hear this, but there is one sure fire method and one absolute cure-all in dealing with the darkness. Read your Bible daily! It is a **CODEX, or code,** and the potency of the vibration of the Word of God causes demons, not only to vacate your presence, but they will absolutely run from you. Dark energies cannot handle the formulated vibration of the Bible. Those of you who are dealing with teens who are being targeted by lower worlds and anyone else who is experiencing attacks, get a Bible and read it. You don't have to even comprehend the context for it to be an effective shield. Allow the Bible to fall open right after you have said a prayer and set your intentions. When you allow the angels and the Holy Spirit to guide you as to what to read, you will find it highly effective as a tool for clearing. Consider also that you must be on a very special path to even be targeted by the lower worlds. They only pick on those who are a direct threat to their existence, those of increased light. Consider it a compliment then make peace with the fact that it is just a part of the process of spiritually evolving. And whatever you do, stay neutral and do not fear them. Fear only enhances the attack. Do your best to stay centered and don't react.

Over the years I have had to battle my own share of these rather boorish creatures and there is another definitive way to rid yourself of them. Send love to them, you heard me correctly, send them "God's highest, purest love and beams of quantified light!" The lower worlds run from warmth and love but more importantly, when you couple pure beams of white light with their intention of promoting and perpetuating fear, those beams become a sword, wielding the highest vibrations in the universe. Don't send them "your" love, you send them God's highest and most concentrated love and light in combination and they will flee from you. There is also a power mantra you can invoke in those moments when fear begins to rise or you get startled out of your sleep by things that go bump in the night. It is an ancient phrase found in the Bible, the Kabbalah and a host of other sacred texts and in English it means, "Holy, Holy, Holy to the Lord God of Hosts/Armies." It is the most powerful phrase in the universe when spoken in the Hebrew tongue, *"Kodoish, Kodoish, Kodoish, Adonai Tsebayoth."* When invoked repeatedly, it not only acts a protection mantra, but it will help you raise your vibrational frequency. I end every meditation with this powerful statement because it sets up a high frequency, vibratory field and it prevents anything dark from entering your inner sanctuary of serenity. Remember that you are in a vulnerable, altered state, when you are meditating.

Did you know that demons walk within the earth and sky?
Did you know they wait upon your anger to arise?
Did you know they love it when you give them food to feed?
Did you know that hate and fear fill all their daily needs?

They cling to you when you have doubt or worry yourself sick
They cling to you when you are lost or when you get heartsick.
They love the suffering of man and use it for their cause
They love to pick on those who're weak and those whose nerves are raw.

They thrive on rage and hateful acts, they wallow in discord
They love to steal the Light of God right from your very core.
You must be strong, stay in The Word and let God be your guide
You must be kind and purposeful and try hard not to deride.

Fill your house with holy things like angels and incense
Fill your house with Higher Love and use some common sense.
Moderation in the use of all which earth gives you
Moderation in all things like alcohol and food.

Pray and meditate each day to offset lower thoughts
Focus on the things you have and what the Lord has brought.

Fill your heart with love and light and practice everyday
To be one with archangels and with the Lord Yahweh.

"There is an ongoing battle for your soul ...feed the Light."

In 2009, I began my foray into social media. At first I was very reluctant and wondered what to tweet and like many, wondered if anyone would care. The first few months were rather dull since I had very few followers. Gradually, I discovered I could synopsize my tidbits of poetic consciousness and tweet them two lines at a time. Then to my surprise, I realized that I was one of the only people on Twitter willing to use the word "God" or tweet a prayer request. In fact, I would put money on the fact that I was one of the first people to tweet a prayer request on large events like bombings, earthquakes, and the passing of pinnacle figures.

I soon found my stride and began meeting people and as my numbers began increasing, I found a new place to share my music from a CD I'd previously recorded a few years earlier. Within three months of tweeting, the United Nations called. Within days of that, suddenly, I found myself, being bullied by a group of catty, shallow, insecure women along with a few men. I absolutely adore women but the one thing I do not abide by is jealousy. It is such a primitive emotion and one I refuse to subscribe to. So I was mortified and stunned at this lot, since I had no idea that people who had never met you, could fabricate and character assassinate with such convincing flair. I realize it happens to actual celebrities everyday, but I was absolutely confounded that it would happen on Twitter! Social media was relatively new in 2009 and the rules of play were, at best, non-existent and sadly, remain so today.

I was devastated with every post, blog, and video these dark souls shared with millions on a daily basis for seven long, excruciatingly painful months. The Holy Spirit kept reciting the same message every single day to me over and over again, "Don't react, don't respond." The more I did not reply or respond, the angrier they seem to become. I will tell you that the Holy Spirit and I went a good three rounds on this one but inevitably, as always, I abide by my higher guidance. I prayed for answers and the only thing the angels assured me of was that if I continued to take the high road and not react or respond, there would be a spiritual reward, when and if I survived it, that is. There were days that some of the lies were so horrendous and abhorrent that I actually entertained thoughts of suicide on more than one occasion but I have never been one to run away from anything and was not about to start now. Still, a woman in her 50's seemed like a very lame target to hate upon, which blatantly revealed the kind of people these were.

I was bullied as a child because of my dark complexion, which stemmed from my father's family originally coming from Spain and then marrying Native American Indians. The rest of my family was white, white and more white, my own mother having red hair and a very freckled face. She and the remainder of the clan originated from England, Ireland, and Scotland.

The pain of trying to understand or wrap my brain around anyone hating a person just because they exist was so foreign to me. I knew it was common in childhood and sadly in the lives of teenagers but these were grown women and men in their 40's and 50's! I could never have imagined that people who appeared to be self-respecting could be so willing to humiliate and degrade themselves in such a public venue, but they did with gleeful evil. These were people I did not personally know though I had actually taken a phone call from one of them. On two separate occasions within two weeks, she was in dire straits and called to ask me to pray with and for her. She actually wrote this beautiful blog after her free session and hearing me pray.

The pain of trying to understand or wrap my brain around anyone hating a person just because they exist was so foreign to me. I knew it existed in childhood and sadly in the lives of teenagers but these were grown women and men in their 40's and 50's! I could never have imagined that people, who appeared to be self-respecting, could be so willing to humiliate and degrade themselves in such a public venue, but they did with gleeful evil. These were people I did not personally know though I had actually taken a phone call from one of them. On two separate occasions within two weeks, she was in dire straits and called to ask me to pray with and for her. She actually wrote a beautiful blog about me after her free "session" and hearing me pray. She was moved to the core and stated that for the very first time in her life, she felt it, something greater than the two of us that afternoon. She went on to say that it was at that moment that she knew for the first time in her life that God really did exist and knew that I had been placed in her life to help her come to that powerful conclusion.

Imagine how daunting it was that someone who authored such a beautiful blog, whom I had shown kindness to and actually helped, suddenly became my worst nightmare. But you see, it wasn't about me, it wasn't me that she hated, it wasn't me the others she enjoined hated; they hated themselves. Their battle had nothing to do with me. In fact, their battle was within, which often is the worst kind of battle.

I am always surprised at the new, weak willed stragglers' who jump into the hate rhetoric, especially those who appeared to have seeming integrity before they lowered themselves to this level of bottom feeding consciousness. I have openly told my followers and fans that if I see anyone bullying anyone or even hating on those who have bullied me, I will still block them.

I will never align my light to that kind of degradation nor will I lower my own light or compromise my integrity for anyone. You have to love yourself enough to see everything as a blessing and to participate only in that which feeds your soul. Every action from another is an opportunity for you to evolve and grow as a spiritual being and human being! Your reactions determine if you gain more light or reduce your own. Will you live it perfectly every time? No, I have my very human moments too, but the goal is to keep those moments to a minimum.

"Persecution is nothing more than a compliment to those who work in the Light"

The earth is full of people all shine so differently
Many hide their darker side so others do not see
Out of nowhere comes the day when shadows rise in them
And you may be the target at the receiving end.

Be aware that you will not be loved by everyone
Be cognizant that you are doing work which must be done
For if you play your role right, many you will see
Will attack you just for being light, and you will ask "Why Me?"

Consider it a compliment when darkness pervades you
For light will be triumphant ore the battle when it's through
No weapon formed against you, no evil will succeed
Be at peace with who you are and let the LIGHT take lead.

Today remember it isn't personal.

"Your actions can be the difference in whether you are a blessing or a liability."

Through almost four years of being a target of bullies in social media, there is a very common chord that runs through many of these people. Many who participate in bullying today are legitimate sociopaths. Sociopaths are people who know how to charm, lie, hate, hurt and repel others because they have no internal gauge that what they are doing is wrong. You only have to watch one of Dr. Phil McGraw's shows to gain a clearer understanding. There are a host of teenagers threatening to kill their families, cheating husbands and boyfriends who have had innumerable affairs, stalkers who go to great lengths to hunt someone down and "catfish," people who create a false identity and then bait the most vulnerable people, conning them out of all of their savings while proclaiming to love them. With rare exception, these kinds of people display sociopathic behavior.

A sociopath's behavior cannot be cured since it is a form of mental illness, so no matter how hard you try, you cannot fix them. Sociopaths usually have a troubled childhood, mommy or daddy damage, use or have abused drugs and alcohol, have a history of bad behaviors and are typically unable to hold a job and can be dangerous. The traits of a sociopath are many; they have superficial charm, grandiose self-worth, a need for stimulation or are prone to boredom They are experts at pathological lying, they are also conning and manipulative with a lack of remorse or guilt, are usually very shallow. They are emotionally limited in their ability to feel at deeper levels and yet can be very gregarious. They are also callous and lack empathy, have promiscuous sexual behavior or are excessively flirtatious and are always very clandestine in their behavior. They are low in their ability to function in a work or office environment and are usually financially dependent on others. Another trait is verbal aggression or the inability to control their temper. They usually are very impatient and prone to irritability and threats. Most sociopaths displayed early behavioral problems prior to age 13 such as lying, theft, bullying, drugs, alcohol, as well as sniffing glue. They are impulsive and irresponsible and typically lack realistic, long term goals.

If you think that having spiritual psychic awareness can ferret these people out, you are sorely mistaken. You see psychic awareness is based on the principle that the person you are reading has a right/wrong barometer internally, thus your psychic senses can pick up on their deception. But with a clinical sociopath, they do not have that barometer. They will look you square into the eye and lie with all the conviction of O.J Simpson himself. They simply do not understand that they have done anything wrong or that their behavior is anything less than typical. Many, who are over forty and freshly divorced, have encountered these types of men and women on dating sites and in social media and sadly, often only after being played like a fiddle.

Social media is a great place for sociopaths because they can hide behind a computer screen and their erratic behaviors will probably never be detected. When I began to really look at the people who were creating the discord, I realized how many of them fit the actual clinical definition of a sociopath. That is when I began to truly understand that this was a part of a greater spiritual process for me. I was learning not to judge others and learning to have compassion for those who are functioning under circumstances which are vastly different than my own.

After seven long months of verbal assaults, I found my salvation in remaining silent all the while praying for the twenty or so who were leading the pack. Through it all I prayed for them, sending them love and even blessing them. Why? Because they are the very people who need prayer the most. These are the very souls whose hate, lies and deceptions, I would use as a launching pad and the catalyst to reach a higher level of consciousness. At the end of the seven months and on my birthday no less, a beautiful glowing blue light began shining from my third eye and crown. It was so visible to the naked eye that my friends eagerly snapped pictures and we all marveled at the beauty of the crystal blue color. As I had been guided to not respond to these adult haters, I found a creative outlet. I poured my dismay out on paper for all those who have known the heartache of being bullied. I drew strength with every word I wrote and to this day, I still gain even more courage with every read of the following poem.

I soar just like an angel as I spread love through the world,
I spread my wings and soar each day in loving flight I twirl.
My gaze falls on all people for they each hold beauty's light,
My prayers extend unto all and everybody's plight

I do not judge the angry ones who try to bring me down
One wing they may have broken, yet God lifts me off the ground,
I will keep spreading my light and shine it on their souls,
I will keep praying for them for darkness love extols

I bless all those who love me but more the ones who hate,
I thank them for the buffet for they are dining from my plate.
I must be someone special to garner their attentions,
I must have struck a chord in these who lift my name in mentions.

I soar just like an angel as I spread Gods love around,
I love folks with abandon none will ever take me down.
No weapon formed against me ever will succeed,
For love is mightier than dark with LOVE I'll always lead.
The universe was created with opposite polarities, without darkness there can be no LIGHT.

"The Divine Return"

Many on the spiritual path are familiar with the, "Life and Teachings of the Masters of the Far East". It's a six-volume set of books which was written by Baird T. Spalding and was published in the early 1930's. Immediately following my death experience in Austria, Jesus appeared on a regular basis during my early morning meditations. We lived in sunny Encino, California at the time and had a beautiful backyard filled with a huge, fruit-bearing orange tree, a pomegranate tree, a lemon tree, a pumpkin patch and a very tasty plum tree. It seemed serendipitous since Jesus's favorite fruit is pomegranate.

My husband had designed a beautiful, perfectly dimensional, copper tube pyramid for me to meditate in. One early Saturday morning, I was in a deep, very powerful meditation when Jesus appeared but this time, it was a little different. I was accustomed to seeing him every morning and it was always so comforting, not to mention mesmerizing. His energy is so loving, so all consuming that you meld into a symbiotic oneness so permeating, you do not want to open your eyes. He is also a very handsome man at 6'4" tall, with his hypnotic ocean blues eyes, which seem to lovingly pierce your soul. He speaks telepathically, so his lips never move and yet you hear the sound of his voice with blazing clarity. It is a voice that resounds so audibly, you feel it all the way to the bone. He has a very dry sense of humor and can be very direct. In the past, he has made me feel very humbled, yet incredibly empowered and always awe-inspired.

Normally, I would see him in my third eye and we would acknowledge each other with a smile and sending beams of telepathic love to one another, then the vision would dissolve. But there were other times when, in broad daylight, he would appear in a full golden apparition, which always brought me to my knees.

I remember him showing up vividly when I was in an angelic cycle in the summer of 1997. An angelic cycle lasts anywhere from 30-90 days. It is a heightened state of awareness where you not only see angels in full apparitions but all of your senses are heightened to such a profound degree, that they are functionally supernatural. In this particular process, (I had been through many) I was asked to remove meat, sugar, caffeine and nicotine from my diet. I had no problem with that until my guides and Spirit told me it had to be done in one day! I had been a cigarette smoker since I was a teenager so quitting in one day was like asking me to part the Red Sea!

Needless to say, I was a little on edge and early that morning for the first time ever, I snapped at my husband when he asked me to do something. I had always been so kind and jovial so to see me persnickety, was strange for him to say the least. Little did I know, it was about to come back to me in a way which taught me more than a thousand books could. The higher you go, the less you get away with anything even a mild infarction like having a bad day. Since I had to withdraw from Nicotine without the benefits of aids like nicotine gum and patches, I resorted to chewing pink bubble gum. I did not know at the time it was also a spiritual no-no since it disrupts your energy fields, but needless to say, I soon found out.

I was in a meditation at four in the afternoon when suddenly Jesus was standing before me. He had the half chewed pack of Bubble Yum in his left hand and as he held it up for me to see, he suddenly closed his hand in what sounded like the gates of heaven slamming shut! Next, he held his right hand out extending a plum he had found in my fruit bowl. I said, "Okay I get it, you want me to stop chewing gum and eat the natural sugar of the plum instead but did you have to be so stern?" His crystal blue eyes looked right through me and with a captivating smile, like a divine branding rod, he seared his telepathic words into my heart forever, "Ariaa", he said, "I am just a reflection of you." I tell you that I truly wanted to crawl under the bed, embarrassed from knowing he had seen me snap, even mildly, at my husband. You don't realize how our behaviors on earth are perceived in the heavens, until you have a monumental moment like that one.

As the sun rose over a smog-covered day in the San Fernando Valley, I was waning from experiencing things on the earth I did not understand. Right after my death experience, after spending what felt like an eternity on the other side with what I have come to term as "the boys", I was like a child with a newly born pure heart and spirit and everything daunted me. We lived in Encino on a busy road and even though I had lobbied for a four-way stop sign to slow traffic down, cats, dogs, ducks and squirrels were being mowed down on a daily basis. I could not understand how travelers could be so self-absorbed and disregarding of nature, that they could not take even sixty seconds to slow down. I cannot tell you how many furry babies I lost tears over and buried. I just could not wrap my brain around certain facets of human behavior.

On this hot California morning, Jesus or as I refer to him, Jehoshua, had something to convey to me. He stood before me, in his full golden glory. His words became as flowing and smooth as liquid gold, painting my soul and flooding my mind; "Get, "The Life and Teachings of the Masters of the Far East and read them". He continued, "Remember who you are." I instantly felt like Simba in the "Lion King!" Remember who I am? You would think that after more than 2000 years he would have expanded his dialogue beyond parables by now! I had been told the same information from the angels and the Holy Spirit for weeks now and yet had not been compelled to run to the store and drop $40.00 dollars on books, when my husband and I lived on a rather modest income at the time. I came to understand far later that when Jesus said "remember who you are," he was of course, talking about the energy that lives within all human beings known as the "Christ" energy, connotative of your perfection. The very awareness and acknowledgement of your complete perfection, heightens the alchemy of mastery.

The mysticism I live and breathe in every area of my life, prepared me for what came next. Within minutes of finishing my meditation and this conversation with Jehoshua, the doorbell rang. Standing at my front door, was a man I met when I lectured at the Brain and Mind Symposium in Los Angeles a few months earlier. He announced that Spirit had sent him over to do a Kabbalah tarot reading on me and as we sat down at the kitchen table, it was as if I was in an episode of the "Twilight Zone." Suddenly his voice changed and in Jesus's voice he repeated verbatim, everything Jesus told me ten minutes earlier in that very private conversation! There was so much more to our morning talk which I did not reveal here and yet Jeff knew all of it!

I ran like Sybil into the backyard and screamed in a befuddled shrill, "OK! I will get the books!" Despite feeling like a stranger in a strange land with all these wondrous spiritual gifts, even I get freaked out by the mystical happenings of my daily life. That day, I got the books and I have never put them down. From the moment I began reading them, I began recommending them at every lecture, to thousands of clients and participants. Within one year there was such a surge in sales that the publisher put together a sixth volume, due to the influx of inquiries DeVorss was getting about the author and his whereabouts. Instantly, the books flew off the shelves when it appeared they had lain dormant for quite some time before these events took place.

In those wise and very profound books, this technique is spoken of. There is a way taught by the masters to deal with those who wish you harm or who are persecuting you in any way. It is a tool that if used improperly, real harm can be done, so readers pay attention and beware. Revenge and the energy of retaliation cross universal law, so when using this technique you need to be very cognizant of your emotions and what your intentions are. If you harbor any ill will toward your intended target it is best you DO NOT IMPLEMENT this technique until such a time when you can come from a heart of pure love. It is the definitive and divine way to deal with those who are sending you negative thoughts or energy.

You are a light generator capable of using the beams of light which emanate from you, as power. Everything is vibration and when you call forth the "Christ perfection" within you, you align yourself to the Divine flow of the ONE. The only reasons people experience anything other than love and flow, is that they have lowered their vibration from the Source Vibration or Principle of Light and Love. When you allow your body to collect and magnify energy, it becomes power and mass in the form of white beams of amplified love and light. You can send this divine power, coupled with all the negative energy, those you perceive as your enemies or those who are trying to harm you are sending to you, even if you don't know them personally or know where they are located. You can pulsate the light to such a high frequency that any resistance they have in receiving quantified love and light, will cause their negative actions encased by divine light, to magnify and increase in such velocity, that the karma returned is compounded. You are only returning their intentions multiplied with light and love and it can be very effective, so long as you are working with the love and light principle and are coming from a pure heart. If your intention is to bring them harm, that limiting thought will cause a quickened amplified return to you and you will in essence, destroy yourself. If they receive these pure beams of light and love you are sending to them, it will pour through you, into them and create a healing for both of you.

Next time you have an issue with anyone, instead of getting angry or even, try getting centered and calm and begin to call forth the Christ Light within you. The longer you call it forth, the greater it magnifies. Close your eyes and see everything the other person is sending to you; anger, judgment, false accusations, lies and resentments and multiply that energy 10 x 10 x 10. Now take that ball of energy they have directed at you and encase it in God's highest purest love and light and multiply that encapsulated ball of energy, 10 x 10 x 10; then send it right back to the same person who directed at you. See that light reaching them and pouring into their third eye, crown and heart chakras. Be certain that you are sending nothing but pure love and pure light.

For years I have told people that I work with and on "beams of light." In fact it is my signature and has been for more than twenty years, *"With Beams of Love, Light and Laughter"*. In my work whether utilizing light as a healing tool, as a "resurrection tool", or as a pain reliever, I amp up the light that comes through me and those pure "God-beams" vibrate at such a high frequency, they actually accomplish whatever the intention is. When you use the principles of the universe, you are working within the universal one of high vibrational flow. Everything was created in perfection and all are vibrating in perfect harmony and accord until they resist the foundation of who they are. Jesus' words to me, "Remember who you are," were a direct beam of encoded wisdom, to remember to align and stay constantly in this frequency of light and embody the divine love principle. The only separation from you and the Creator Light, God, Divine Mind, is the resistance to this divine principle which causes imbalance, thus taking you out of the flow of harmony.

The Mountain's Echo
Ask, Speak, Find

"Listen for I'll tell you that there is no great truth, if you say to the mountain go, the mountain shall be moved."

In nearly twenty-one years of private practice, I have seen just about everything from substance and sexual abuse to health and low self-esteem in my clients. Many times the first thing a client will ask me is "Why did this happen", or "Why can't I fix my life?" The answer is plain and simple. It begins with the most basic formula. You have to pose that very question to the universe in a sincere and potent way which will generate the answer. The amount of energy you pour into anything determines the amount of energy which will return to you. Most people forget to consult their guides and angels and most fail to meditate so they can uncover the answers!

One of the many reasons I am so effective at moving mountains and shifting circumstances in other people's lives, is because I COMMAND those mountains to move. It goes back to the scripture, "Ask and it is given, seek and ye shall find, knock and the door is opened unto you". In my case I go far beyond asking. I work within the by-laws of the universe and additionally I work with three core elements, energy, consciousness, and knowing.

Energy becomes more potent when intention is added into the equation. Thus with enough intention anything is possible because your intent continues to multiply and magnify the energy. Consciousness is a little more complex because everyone is operating at a different level of consciousness. The more evolved your consciousness or awareness, the more you begin to look at things from a higher, non-emotional perspective and with a broader vision. The more evolved you are, the more you want to know. If more people would go within and would pose their issues to "spirit," they would discover what the real reason is for the physical manifestation. If more would seek to understand and take responsibility for every drama which unfolds in their lives, the results would be higher solutions from Spirit and the lasting resolve would manifest in their lives.

Self-realization is a process by and which you examine, heal, and integrate all those aspects and characteristic flaws which prevent you from living a life in peace and with joy. But you have to understand yourself to heal, integrate and transform your life. There is a reason for every event and everything under the sun. Spiritual processing, as many of you know, can be both a blessing and a curse. The blessings are obvious. You gain greater spiritual gifts, you clear or integrate cellular memories, you can audibly hear your angels and even see them if you are gifted with spiritual sight. The bad news is, that many times processing is very painful and very few will tell you how challenging some of these processes can be.

"Pardon me, I am just transmuting."

I have gone through weeks of kundalini processing and angelic cycles where I slept for days only rising to eat a peach, then falling back into a deep sleep for as many as five days at a time. Most people don't have the luxury to sleep through the days like that, but I was very fortunate to work from home on a schedule I created and to have a husband who was wonderfully supportive. You can also ask the universe, your higher self, the angels and the Holy Spirit to regulate your processing, so it does not interfere with your work or daily routine and they will!

In our society, we have been genetically dumbed down over the centuries and have become dependent on limiting beliefs. You hear on the news every day that if you eat this, you will get cancer or have a heart attack, or if you go out into the damp air, you will catch a cold. Most people buy into the fear rhetoric of pharmaceutical companies and political circles, rarely considering they have a monetary agenda. Many have the idea that we must go to war with countries whose cultures and traditions, we have not even begun to embrace much less understand. Society has enabled companies, overzealous pundits and news reporters, to perpetuate limited ideas on those gullible enough to listen, when instead they could be listening to the sages and the wisdom which has been passed down throughout the ages.

"There are no wrong or right paths when searching for the light for they all lead to the same divine door".

It was Jesus himself who said *"Know Ye not that Ye are gods". "Everything I do, can you also do and more".*

It was Buddha who said, *"No one saves us but ourselves. No one can and no one may. We ourselves must walk the path".*

It was Babiji who said, *"Seek the consciousness that we are all one".*

And it was the wonderful teacher, Parmahansa Yogananda, who said, *"Remain calm, serene, always in command of yourself. You will then find out how easy it is to get along."*

Many wise souls have come to this planet and repeatedly emphasized that you have all the power of creation within you, if you awaken and actuate it. I remember in Neale Donald Walsh's book, "Conversations with God" he was talking to "God" and God was telling him that Neale was god and one with all Creation and Neale asked the pinnacle question that most would ask. In a rather sarcastic tone he asked why God had not sent someone to earth to tell us that we are gods. In a surprisingly curt answer, God replied that he had sent many but we (humans) keep killing them. You have got to love that kind of honest profundity!

"There are no greater answers than the ones that lie inside of you."

When you start seeking the answers as to why you act the way you do, why you feel the way you do, why you behave outside of love's divine realm, you will find that the answers begin to unfold. It is imperative that you are ready to hear the answer, for many times it stems from drama or trauma that occurred in another lifetime and you are just acting out based on fear or hurt from those very experiences. Most of what occurs in your life this time around is nothing more than cellular memory being compounded. In other words, the core memory of an injury from another lifetime will create again in this lifetime unless you seek to see and understand why you have the pain today. Many just run to the doctor failing to see how empowering it is to heal yourself by seeking from within and understanding what the ailment is trying to show you. When you have drowned in another life, chances are you will fear it in this one. It's just that simple.

If you had issues with addiction or betrayal in other lifetimes, you may have mastered it or you may repeat it to heal this time around. ***Cellular memory is the "imprint" of past lifetime experiences written in your flesh.*** When your soul came to this earth and was born into this body, you came with consciousness and memories. What you have lived and experienced in another period of time, especially those things which were impactive to your spirit or flesh, you imprint it into your new body. Some memories are stronger than others. Typically the ones which caused you the greatest pain or damage, are those which you are back to heal or grow from.

If you do not ask the questions in this lifetime as to why you feel or act a certain way, if you don't seek to understand yourself and take full responsibility for all you are encountering, then these memories may cause you to feel like a victim. Most people do not want to do as the sages taught. Most don't want to be god and one with God because it means they can't blame anyone else for their lot in life. They simply don't want that much responsibility and would often rather go through life blind to the reasons for their pain, heartache, and loneliness.

I had a client once who was so afraid of losing her children that it bordered on paranoia. It was far outside the lines of a mother's normal concern for her children. Using several modalities over a period of just a few weeks, I was able to help her uncover that she had lost 8 children in Ireland to a sudden fire in the 1700's. She not only saw the event but she was able to embrace that many of those same souls who had been her children before, returned to her life today, in the form of friends and family.

You see no one ever leaves us, we all return to each other time and time again. I am emphatic about helping people uncover their own memories and utilize hard and true techniques which unveil those memories in such a way that my clients are able to digest and work through the trauma as opposed to locking it up again emotionally.

I had a client many years ago who for reasons she could not find, was unable to bond with a man and was unable to be completely happy. She had money, she was beautiful, she was a kind and good person and she had a very fulfilling career but she simply was unhappy and found fault with every man she dated. When I did my first "body scan" on her, I instantly saw the face of a man, very distinct. He was young and good looking and had features which were unique. I saw him standing over a crib and saw that he touched his young daughter inappropriately when she was just a baby no more than 12 months old. He did not do this was malice or some sort of deviant behavior; he looked and touched, simply because he had never seen a baby girls' private parts before and he was curious. What Lisa could not see as a baby she felt instantly; these two people had a past life encounter which was abusive and sexual so that harmless moment felt far differently and was more traumatic to her soul, even though she was only a baby.

I did not reveal what I had seen in my third eye but instead, employed some of my own spiritual gifts and applied several techniques guaranteed to help her remember those events on her own. Unlike many psychically gifted personalities today, I do not like to "tell" a person their own lifetimes when I can instead, cause them to see it on their own. I don't wish to rob anyone of their personal power, so by using my gifts to generate the clients own ability to see into their past and present, they are better able to integrate the memories and digest the information.

Three days later, my client Lisa returned to my home for a follow up appointment and she came with pictures. Not only had her memories surfaced but what she had to tell me, validated what I had seen. She handed me a picture of her father who had died a long suffering death to cancer many years earlier. It was exactly the image I had seen in my third eye only days earlier! I do not have a poker face so my mouth gapped wide open! Lisa instantly knew that her father is the one I had seen during her body scan. She continued to share that all of her life there was this "energy" between her and her father and that she loved him very much but always kept her distance because she could not define that underlying "energy" and it made her nervous. She went on to say that when he got sick, she had to take care of him and that she struggled with her senses during that time. It was very hard for her to deal with the odd feelings she was having while he laid there dying, so she simply ignored and compartmentalized them. She had spent the days since our first appointment crying and reconciling all that surfaced as it surfaced, integrating all of the emotions of the past and making peace with them. Four months later, she was in a loving, healthy relationship and everything in her life suddenly improved; she got a promotion at work, a raise, and was head over heels in love.

Nothing heals more powerfully than identifying those lifetimes where your hang-ups and hurts are slowly simmering and hemorrhaging. Every memory has a divine timing and surfaces when you are ready to embrace it. When you begin to explore the depths of your own soul, you will discover things that make such sense, you become more at peace with yourself and your life. Asking the right questions is a definitive way to pull up the answers. Anything you seek is given you when you pour your heart and soul into wanting to know it. But you have to ask.

"The questions are as important as the answers."

In a state of limbo I awoke this day to see
A star which spoke unto my soul, across the sky it streamed.
It was the second morning I'd seen a star shoot by
My soul had asked God questions, the what, the how, the why.
And here I found my answer so simple but profound
A word in luminescence set me on higher ground.

There are times within a life, when stillness pierces light
It shucks you like a stalk of corn and grinds you in the night.
The quiet like a calm which comes before a storm moves in
Feeds a sense of urgency to seek and look again…
Seek the moment's quiet, to capture higher thought
Let the silence take you where your babbling cannot.

The messages will come to you in ways you understand
A star ablaze assured me, that my life was in God's hand.
You have to ask the questions for answers to unfold
You have to be quite vigilant and many times quite bold.
You have to seek with all your heart before the answers come
But trust me when I tell you that God speaks to everyone.

"You are in essence reweaving the fabric of your wholeness, reawakening the remembrance that you were born in perfection and you are returning to complete perfection."

The soul is the very breath of love but not the kind of love you know as human love. The love I speak of goes beyond ego, beyond feeling or your five senses. The kind of love I speak of is all encompassing and is complete in and of itself. It consumes you beyond the scope of comprehension. It is a state of being not a feeling. Anytime you have any reaction outside of the scope of love, like jealousy, fear, anger, doubt, insecurity, there are dynamics and consequences to acting upon those lower human emotions. Of course, they are a good catalyst to grow from, but in order to grow, you have to embrace each scenario which stems from such emoting.

As you begin to ask the questions, you find the answers will surprise you and as you embrace the answers, you find an integration of all your best aspects, which ultimately empowers you. It's as if there are holes in your personality, behavior or character and with each question posed, with each answer given, you heal the spaces in between, within the fabric of love. ***It is not a God outside of yourself who judges you; there is no such animal.*** It is you and you alone, who hold yourself in such contempt for whatever you have done in any lifetime, which has robbed you of completeness and peace. When you embrace the questions, when you take responsibility for whatever you have drawn into your life to learn and grow from, when you begin to understand yourself, the joy and the pure perfection returns.

I urge you to learn to meditate, learn to go within and seek the answers. Next time you get angry in traffic, ask why. The next time you feel jealous of anyone, ask why. The next time you feel fear of any kind, seek to understand that fear, learn to embrace the negative emotions and ask why you are feeling them. And don't just ask once; ask until you get the answers through dreams or meditation. I teach my clients to pray the same question every night before they go to bed until they get the answers. I have them command the angels reveal the records of their own soul, by commanding, "SHOW ME" whatever needs to be seen which will bring forth the greatest healing.

"When answers can no longer be found outside, divine solutions unfold inside."

Remember, the more energy you propel into anything the greater the outcome. I jokingly tell people that one of the reasons I hear the angels and Spirit with such audible clarity is because I hound them until they give me the answer just to hush me up! You have to be persistent and consistent in how and what you seek to know! Your spiritual growth, your life on earth is in your hands. You have to want to heal, you have to want to grow, you have to want to live with pure joy and inner peace. No one can give that to you.

Take your power back because there is no separation from you and Creator. Creator is love beyond love to the one billionth power, you are never separated from that love. The only thing that separates us is the ego. The ego is where all the lower emotions dwell. Beyond the ego is where supreme love resides. Step out of the ego and into the paradisiacal realm of living a life in pure love. As you navigate the oceans of consciousness shifting, you will encounter every emotion the human body is capable of conceiving. You will rise to great peaks and plunge to great depths, that is to be expected. But remember, that it is only a part of the greater reward. The grander reward is freedom from all limiting emotions and circumstances.

"It is the wise person who understands the phrase, "This too will pass" because is always does."

Have you ever looked back on the dramas of your life?
And seen that in your striving through the crying and the strife?
All the drama passed you by and a calm surrender came;
Everything worked out just fine like sunshine after rain.

The less emotions you emote brings instant clarity,
The greater calm that you maintain brings synchronicity.
It's like a stone you skip across the waters of your mind,
The smaller that you make them, the ripples quicker will subside.

If you flail and fold under a full dramatic siege,
Suffering and misery will soon follow your lead.
If you sit and dwell in peace and reflect inwardly,
The Light will fill the darkness with a profound energy.

The energy of knowing that your heart is cared for too,
The energy of wisdom and solutions come to you.
The energy of comfort for the wounds within your soul,
The energy of renewal will come and make you whole.

I tell you there is nothing richer than with God attuned,
To be at one with love and light and let that fill the room.
You cannot be deceived when first you discipline through peace,
The answers will reclaim you as you take a quantum leap.

The Wisdom of the Sages Beyond the Veil

"There is wisdom in stillness...be still."

Meditation in its truest form has been medically proven to reduces stress, improve sleep and increase awareness. It also lowers the pulse and heart rate and gives the body a chance to reclaimate and restore itself. A 2007 study by the U.S. government found that nearly 9.4% of U.S. adults (over 20 million) had practiced meditation and since then the numbers have nearly doubled.

The word meditate comes from the Latin root meditatum, which means to ponder. In the Old Testament the Hebrew word Haga means to sigh or murmur, but also to meditate. When the Hebrew Bible was translated into Greek, hāgâ became the Greek, melete. The Latin Bible then translated hāgâ/melete into meditation.

Since the 1960s, meditation has been the focus of increasing scientific research. In over one thousand published research studies, various methods of meditation have been linked to changes in metabolism, blood pressure, brain activation, and other bodily processes. Meditation has been used in clinical settings as a method of stress and pain reduction as well. Meditation has many medical benefits including lowering your blood pressure and slowing down your heart and pulse rate. Meditation also gives your body a chance to recover from stress, noxious fumes, and every day activity, both mentally and physically. When you meditate, preferably a chakra meditation, you align all your core energy centers and ground light, peace, tranquility and love from within. Meditation gives your body the ability to reset to optimal performance and every twenty minute meditation, is equivalent to a two hour nap.

Adding meditation to your routine brings many positive physical, mental and spiritual benefits. Meditation is common in Buddhism, Taoism, Hinduism and Sikhism and Christianity. Meditation is sometimes used for healing purposes. Even Atheists and Agnostics have been known to meditate. It is becoming more common in medicine as a way to reduce pain and stress, and has positive effects on the respiratory and cardiovascular systems. In essence, mediation is essential whether you are on a spiritual path or not. There are also medical meditations, strictly for enhancing health and well-being.

As spiritual beings we meditate as a way of connecting with and bringing in the high light of God. We become still and quiet, aligning with that perfect self, the pure essence of Godness or goodness within each human being. You, along with help from the Creator light, your angels, and your guides, divined and designed what your life's journey and purpose would be, before you ever came to the earth to live it out. You stay attuned to that higher aspect, if you go with the flow of your life by meditating and by utilizing prayer power, and a heart full of love and intention. Love quickens and accelerates divine flow and everything else in your life. One way to hone your intentions and desires is through meditation. Prayer is how we speak to Divine Mind or the Universe. Meditation is how we listen, attuning to the high light of God, as we receive guidance from the angelic realm. When you let go of your ego and quiet your mind, when you stop emitting, thoughts and higher wisdom can flow in.

When you first begin to meditate, I encourage you to just focus on you. Sit for a few minutes and breathe deeply as you attune your energy to the divine energy flowing into your crown chakra at the top of your head. Just let go and allow yourself the freedom to do nothing but inhale and exhale in rhythm. Breathe deeply through your nostrils, expanding your lungs and hold to the count of four.

ONE...

TWO...

THREE...

FOUR...

Now exhale through your mouth and blow all of that breath out where your chest becomes concave. Again, repeat the process. The more you oxygenate your cells, the more relaxed you will become. Deep breathing accelerates the calming process and the idea of meditation is to relax and become immersed in the light, allowing every physical process to reset to a more perfect rhythm. A daily meditation will renew, recharge, and re-energize your body, mind and soul and you will be ready to take on the day with joyful enthusiasm.

While in meditation, your posture is the key to raising your vibrational frequency and aligning to the light feed which pours into you from the top of your head all the way down into your ground chakra. If you slump or sit back on your buttocks, you can effectively retard your own spiritual processing. The key then is to sit up straight and upright with your back straight, your head level, and your pelvic floor touching the chair you're sitting on. You may need to tilt forward ever so slightly to achieve the perfect meditation posture. Whatever you do, do not ever lie down to meditate. Meditation is an altered state of consciousness and laying down leaves you vulnerable to lower energies.

"Breathe deeply and let calm clarity engulf you, for in the silence angels whisper and divine solutions unfold."

In my own work I have used meditation to prepare clients for surgery, to deal with bipolar disorder, eating disorders, addiction, and depression. It has also been instrumental in helping others gain awareness, lose weight, reduce their blood pressure, to induce sleep and to relieve pain. It is also the definitive gateway to spiritual awakenings and evolution. My counseling sessions typically end with prayer and a twenty minute meditation as I have seen the results work time and time again. When a client is emoting, upset over their problems or an issue, it is rare that solutions will be found. It is in the calm quiet that higher solutions reveal themselves.

There are many ways to meditate and in fact, many of my gentlemen clients tell me they get into a form of meditation while running. A "runners high is for many, a way to think and release stress. There are meditations utilizing music or staring at a singular object such as a leaf or candle flame. There are toning meditations using Tibetan bowls or indigenous drums and even Yoga and Tai chi are forms of meditation. However, true meditation does not involve thinking at all, quite the contrary. True meditation is silent, calm quiet. I call it, "flat-lining" the brain waves because that is precisely what you are doing. I tell my clients that if they are furrowing their brow, their brain waves are active. Yogis in India have been studied over the years and when they are in a deep state of meditation, their brain waves are practically flat on a cat scan.

Many find it difficult to empty out their thoughts and let go of their ego but practice is the key to refining and honing meditation in order to reach new heights of awareness. Additionally, deep steady breathing, oxygenating the cells and relaxing the muscles, slows down the pulse and heart rate. I have my clients use the mantra "peace, be still," because you are giving the brain a direct order or command and whatever you tell your brain, your body responds to. When you breathe deeply you inevitably succumb to peace. Not only can you add years to your life but the wisdom you are able to then access makes the effort of learning to meditate all the more worthwhile.

I would like to expand a little on one kind of meditation, as I believe it is one of the most powerful avenues to healing, energizing and aligning the mind, body, spirit to the higher light. Obviously my work is spiritually based so light and love are the foundation of my meditations because they are so power enhancing. When you align your body, mind and spirit to these two core elements, you are attuned to the highest rhythm in the universe because all of creation is comprised of these two core elements. So it makes sense that whatever you tell your mind, your body will align itself to as well. As a soul you are comprised of love and when you act outside of love there are consequences. Meditation is one definitive way to realign to the flow in all creation, the infinite well of love.

Chakra mediation originated in Hinduism, but today, has spread far and wide. It is being implemented by all walks of life, sans religion. Additionally, chakras are used in Ayurveda medicine for healing. There are seven main energy centers called the chakras in the human body. I recommend a daily chakra meditation, as I find it's benefits to be indisputable when it comes to emotional and physical healing. Meditation is used to open and release blockages that are believed to be linked to disease. Each of the energy chakras in the body is also believed to relate to the health of various aspects of the body. Appearing like energetic spinning wheels, they allow energy to flow from one part of the body to another and they govern certain organs and emotions. Chakra means "wheel" in Sanskrit and consciousness and energy move from one frequency to another in a spiraling fashion. There are seven primary chakras, all denoted by color and attuned to musical notes. Let's take a moment to touch upon each one, though there are many good books about chakras, which elaborate far greater on all of the emotional and healing benefits associated with working in these powerful centers. I highly recommend you pick one up.

- ⚛ The 1st chakra is red and is located at the base of the spine. It represents fight or flight and human will and governs the kidneys and adrenal glands. It grounds us in the physical world.

- ⚛ The 2nd chakra is orange and is located in the womb or abdominal area and represents feelings of sexual guilt, feelings of being unproductive or non-creative. It governs the reproductive system. Blockage manifests as emotional problems or sexual guilt.

- ⚛ The 3rd chakra is yellow and is located in the solar plexus. It is the seat of emotions and the center of ego and power issues, fear of loss or emotional hurt. It governs the stomach gall bladder, spleen and liver, all part of the digestive tract and the ability to digest life's demands. It gives us a sense of personal power in the world. Blockage manifests as anger or a sense of victimization.

- ⚛ The 4th chakra is the heart chakra and is green. It is the core energy for all issues of love, trust and security. It is the center through which we give and receive love and forgiveness. It governs the heart, blood and circulatory systems. Blockages manifest as heart problems such as hardening of the arteries, heart attack, or arrhythmias.

- ⚛ The 5th chakra is blue and is the throat chakra. It is the center of expression and communication and how we perceive others in their self-expression. It is also the center of wisdom and judgment and by healing this energy center you release resentments, disappointments and feelings of repression. This powerful center governs the lungs, bronchial tubes and throat.

⚜ The 6th chakra is indigo and is called the "third eye". It is located right between the eyes and is our visualization center. It is your direct link into higher vision or perception. This power chakra when activated becomes like a TV screen for the Divine. Here you can see beyond the mundane into the extraordinary worlds of creation. It governs the pituitary gland and brain functions.

⚜ The 7th chakra is known as the crown chakra and is located at the top of the head right above the 3rd eye. It is the highest integration of the human form merged with God. It connects you with Spirit and enables you to receive telepathic messages from angels, guides and Spirit. Here you are awakened to a heightened degree of awareness and what once looked difficult becomes a non-issue. A broader and less emotional perspective is available here. It governs the pituitary and pineal glands.

When you block the flow of energy, or Chi, within your body, health issues arise. Beginning your day with the right intention, centering and aligning yourself to love, peace, tranquility and high light, just makes good sense. You are equally aligning yourself to your angels and guides. Would you take your car out without putting gas in it? Of course not. So why take your body into this chaotic world every day without filling it with light and aligning it to pure love and peace-filled calm? Beginning your day with clarity, with guidance and centeredness, will increase your productivity and enhance your life's experiences. I highly encourage you to learn to meditate and don't get discouraged if it takes you several tries to get it right. Meditation is a discipline and once mastered, it is the gift that keeps giving throughout your entire lifetime.

"The gift is only as good as the receiver."

Take just a moment to close your eyes and quiet your thinking mind. Reach up with one hand and feel your forehead. If you are furrowing your brow, then your brain waves are active. The idea is to "flat line" the brainwaves through deep breathing and stillness. If you need a mantra to stop thinking, simply say to yourself, *"I am at peace,"* or *"peace, be still."* Now, just breathe deeply and loosen your shoulders, allowing the stress to just melt away. Breathe in the peace and let go of anything that is unlike love. Breathe in the following words as a way to just begin centering yourself before you align your chakras and don't forget to begin your meditation by setting your intentions through the spoken word or prayer.

Breathe and surrender to the calm, quiet tranquility and quietly say to yourself:

I am at peace with life and life is at peace with me.

I am provided for and all my needs are met.

I am healthy and my body is renewed and restored each day.

I am blessed and money flows to me in the most extraordinary ways.

I am loved and love surrounds me wherever I go.

I am productive and I accomplish all my goals with great ease and flow.

I am guided and legions of angels surround and assist me each day.

I am at peace with myself and all those in my life.

I am pure love.

I am a magnet for goodness, integrity, honesty, and kindness.

I am a magnet for LOVE and love fills every cell of my body and goes before me and prepares the way.

I am aligned to the highest will for my life and I am attuned to God's highest rhythm.

All is perfect in this moment.

LOVE fills my mind, body and soul and I am at peace.

Peace be still.

> *"Prayer is your direct line to the invisible*
> *to create the visible."*

Prayer is the great communicator not just when there is a crisis, but when you wish to create something or see a dream fulfilled. Most don't recognize how potent the power of prayer is, the power of speaking your heart's desires to the Universe. You might be Jewish, Christian, Hindu, Muslim, or Buddhist, metaphysical, or just on a non-dogmatic, spiritual path, but the good news is, "prayer knows no religion." The point of prayer is that you culminate your energy and intention, while propelling it into the Universe, making your heart and desires known. We co-create our own reality based on many variables. Some you can see, while others remain known only to your highest self.

> *"Open your heart to the needs of others,*
> *and yours too will be filled."*

I like to begin every day with a prayer, praying for everyone and anyone I can think of. I like to pray for those who will never know that I am praying for them. The morning news is full of stories about people in need so why not fulfill that need by praying for them. You set the intention and the tone for the day when you begin by opening your heart. The power of speaking your intentions into the universe is as old as time itself. Prayer not only soothes the soul but as energy, it accomplishes at the same rate as its propellants, energy and intention. When you pray, you are in effect activating the god within and raising your Christ energy, where all answers are aligned and adjoined to the highest will. Using prayer as a way to generate and intensify your intentions just makes sense. You propel all that energy into the Universe, where your angels and guides are waiting to act upon your heart's desires. Why, then, do some of your prayers go unanswered? It's simple, because they are out of alignment with what you originally came to accomplish on this planet, or it may be a matter of bad timing. In other words your prayer may be premature, but eventually, with enough intent, what you prayed for will more than likely manifest. When you pray call forth the "Christ consciousness" within you and raise it higher until you are attuned to God's perfect rhythms.

Christ consciousness is a term many in the spiritual community have used over the past thirty years or so and it has nothing to do with religion or dogma. Christ Consciousness is the merging or fusion of human ego with Divine Mind, where concentric love creates at light speed and brings forth all manifestations held with pure intention. It takes courage, discernment, wisdom and self-respect to realize this level of mastery. This state of being has often been termed "enlightened" in some cultures but it is the living experience of the words of Jehoshua, aka Jesus, when he said, "All things that I do, can ye also do and more". Jesus was of course called, "the Christ" because he achieved a supreme level of selflessness and mastered the art of unconditional love. But, many others like Buddha, Parmahansa Yogananda, Babaji, Krishna and so many more, have also mastered unconditional love and selflessness.

Jesus' role was as God incarnate, or the greatest measure of the Holy Spirit incarnate in one human being. His role was designed to reconcile the ways of man with unconditional love and unconditional forgiveness; in other words, to merge heaven and earth in one body. His role was not only to reconcile these elements but to show us that there is no death and we, as perfect creations, continue on living beyond this earthly plane. His ascension was the ultimate demonstration of the unlimited god potential within all human beings. His heightened purity, selflessness and awareness actually altered his own DNA, enabling him to dematerialize and to ascend. The objective and emphasis of his mission on earth, was and is, that his life personifies what every human being can accomplish.

Perseverance, discipline, diligence, meditation, prayer, and healing the emotions of the past and present, all cultivated, do precisely what Jesus taught and that in turn, internally alters human DNA. When culminated over a period of time, as you undergo a series of spiritual processes, your frequency becomes more love-dominated, thus more liberated, joyful and peaceful. The fear which creates separation from the light and the hart of love, the fear which creates isolation and despair, begins to diminish in thought and feeling as your consciousness rises. Peace begins within and all levels of mastery are dependent upon that inner peace.

How do you attain this level of spiritual and human evolution? There is no one formula to living in fusion or oneness with all the sages and the angelic realm. There are many paths to learning how to hear the higher solutions, see into the worlds beyond, and dwell with one foot in the heavens and one foot in the earth. However balance, moderation, detachment, discernment, persistence, self-discipline and exercising love and kindness in all areas of your life, are a great way to begin. There are additional ingredients to this formula of living in harmony with all. The Ten Commandments are a basic outline of how to move through life with loving oneness but there are also commonsensical by-laws which enhance the human experience. In no particular order they are…

- Love yourself
- Do no harm
- Count your blessings, maintain a grateful heart
- Always remember that everything you do returns to you multiplied
- Heal yourself
- Forgive quickly including yourself
- Forget easily
- Lose yourself in nature
- Kiss babies
- Hug animals
- Honor the elderly
- Embrace every culture
- Celebrate aging
- Relish change, it is inevitable
- Meditate, meditate, meditate

- ⚛ Pray every day, many times a day
- ⚛ All the answers lie within
- ⚛ Covet nothing, cling to no one
- ⚛ Give no value to your possessions, they are temporary
- ⚛ Do not kill anything, everything has a purpose
- ⚛ Get out of yourself at least one day a week and give yourself over to serving others
- ⚛ Leave the door open to your heart only ghosts travel through closed doors*
- ⚛ Remember who you are; YOU are god and one with God.

"Know you not that you are gods?" *~ Jesus, John 10:34*

Soul travelers, why continue searching outside of yourself? You have all the answers deep within at the very core of your soul. You may not know it, but that is the absolute truth. Embrace the simple yet profound truth that every answer to every problem resides within you. You co-authored the outline of your life with your angels and guides, long before you ever came to earth. The universe is divinely designed with multiple layers, also known as parallel universes. Think of it like a filo dough pastry where the good juicy filling is tucked underneath all the light layers of crusty, flakey, dough. Each layer is delicious and the closer you get to the filling, the more tasty it becomes. The Universe is like that.

There are many outcomes for every perceived problem within each parallel universe and the closer you get to the core energy, the highest paradigm, which is Creator, the heart of love, the less consequences there are and the greater the flow. The highest solutions for every area of your life are at the paradigm closest to love. Love centers, it balances, it restores, it heals, it forgives with great ease, it effervesces, it removes limitations, it frees the soul and it renews all things. Love is the answer to every question and every problem. It only needs to be invoked and practiced for it to become first nature when encountering any opposition in life.

"The ego feasts on that which is worthless while the soul feasts on that which is eternal."

The ego is in a constant battle with your higher self, jockeying for the prize, controlling your every thought and move, to keep you locked into living a life in limitation. Some think of the ego as an attribute of arrogance but an ego is the sum total of all your lower emotions. Fear, doubt, judgments, arrogance, insecurity, jealousy, envy, hate, anger, shame, guilt, gloom, sorrow, loneliness, worthlessness, greed and many others are contained within the ego of all human beings. At one time or another in every life, you will feel one or more of these emotions.

As you aspire and reach new levels of soul evolution, you come to recognize the triggers that cause you to react and activate these lower emotions. Wounds from the past in your childhood or another lifetime are normally the culprit. The greatest wisdom comes from knowing yourself and assessing the entirety of your life's experiences. You are not a victim to your moods, your emotions or even your body. You are in control of all of it, you define what to believe and what to dismiss. When you begin to live your life as the creator and inventor of all the circumstances of your life, when you begin to hold yourself accountable for your thoughts, your karma and your actions, when you begin to own what you are attracting into your life, you evolve rapidly.

"There is no greater guru than the one that lies within you."

You are the divine architect of your life and nothing is impossible to you. When you align your earth self to your higher self, when you tune into the highest plateau, that which you divinely designed before you were born into the earth, you manifest the highest and best in every area of your life. If you chose to repay all of your negative karma from several lives, then you will probably feel like a victim in this one, but you aren't a victim. Your perception is elemental to your ability to change and transform your life.

You are master of all that you attract, all that you encounter and all that you create. There is no separation from the Creator Light or Divine Mind until you create one. So the cosmic lesson is basic. Don't create one! The oneness is omnipresent, all-inclusive and all-pervading. Step into your power and out of the notion that you are not in control. That is an illusion and holds not one ounce of truth. There is only one great truth in the universe, and it is, "You are gods."

I am a Divine reflection of everyone and everything around me, the vastness of the universe seared in every cell, in every soul.

I am the Divine amplification of Creator, love beyond measure, love quantified in mass delivery.

I am the Divine Light which feeds the world with unique brilliance, with the effervescence of an atomic glow, with the warmth of a thousand summer winds.

I am you and you are me, molecules and energy reflected as Divine mind, manifested as the purest heart poured into the world as a radiant beam of endless, selfless love.

I am you and you are me in the sunrise and sunset of each other's shadow.

"Everything in the universe responds to love."

Love is science in motion. You only need to say the word over and over again to alter the energy of those around you. It actually alters and changes the molecular structure in all living creation, plant, mineral, water, animal and, human. Love poured into the dark places, raises them to surface, where they can be evaluated and healed. Love added into any scenario is like sugar, it makes everything much easier to digest, no matter what you are going through. How do you do that?

Remember who you are. You are not the sum of your problems and you are not the sum of what others' think of you or say of you. You are the sum of infinite solutions and infinite wisdom which only comes to you when you are still, when you are in a peaceful place. Get out of yourself often, for when you take the focus off of you and use your light and gifts to help others, your own problems begin to shift and dissolve.

Begin your day with meditation or simply sit quietly and breathe in that light. Get centered in the silence and let your mind, body and soul attune to peace, calm, clarity, and love. Be gentle with yourself, let love fill you up inside and let it pour out on others. The more you give, the more you receive. Love encircles and returns to you multiplied. LET IT POUR! Say it, proclaim it, and telepathically send it out every day to everyone and everything as if you are a walking tape recorder. With consistency and passion you will transform the molecular structure of the entire universe. You can move mountains in your own life but more importantly, you can use this newly discovered power to telepathically feed the world and the universe. You may feel silly at first but I tell you that whatever you proclaim becomes so in one way or another. You have nothing to lose and everything to gain!

"Love pours from my heart and my lips are found speaking its radiant hue.

Loves radiance pours into the world into the awaiting arms of all who open theirs.

I meld into its life force and it feeds the hungry world".

The following Ariaaisms, are a great exercise for learning how to use your mind over matter capabilities as well as helping you generate a pure and selfless heart. I do this routinely with my friends in our daily meditation but thought it would be fun to put it in a rhyming format. I encourage you to reach beyond your own personal life into the world and the universe and help to move mountains with your propelled intent and energy. There is nothing as gratifying as creating on a global scale and nothing as enriching as serving without a thought for self. I encourage all to speak it out loud with conviction as you help transform the world. This is a global exercise in the movement of peace.

Today we turn our heads toward a needed energy,
To fill the world with peace and love, a strange anomaly.
Contemplate a peace so still that silence fills the earth
Conjure up a peace profound create a peaceful girth.

Peace be still in all the places where wars loom at large
Peace be still in all the souls who lead the maddening charge.
Peace be raised in hearts and minds and peace be to their souls
Peace come forth and draw all in, restore love in the whole.

I send thoughts of lasting peace, I send great beams of love
I send great calm with hands outstretched to lift the light thereof.
I send forth light across the globe, wherever there's descent
I send forth all the love of God, I am the instrument.

I am at peace with humankind, with the entire world indeed
I am at peace with all strangers and everyone I meet.
I am at peace with ignorant men who hate with no regard
I am at peace with all the carnage left in earths' backyard.

Peace sweet everlasting peace I raise my eyes to God
Peace sweet everlasting light, peace be the lightning rod.
Peace be still all humankind, peace be to the world
In every corner peace supreme is what I now unfurl.

Once again, use your energy with passion and conviction to pour out love on all living creation.

This Ariaaism is a global exercise in the movement of Love.

Today we use our hearts and souls and minds to generate,
Love intense and quantified to remove worldly hate.
Use your hands and arms as rods and lift them to the sky
Say these words aloud with me and state them by and by.
I send love of the highest and the purest yes I do
I send love so magnificent it comes from heaven too.
I send love so intensified, multiplied to the tenth power
I send love so enriched with light it feeds like thunder showers.

Love so sacred, love so real, love so whole, complete
Love illumined and of God, love so richly sweet.
Love unmeasured, love so kind, love times ten times ten
Love sweet everlasting love is the great love that I send.

I send it to all corners of the universe and globe
I send it to all angels in a showering overflow.
I send it to all people and the animals of earth
I send it to the mountains, the seas and morning surf.

I send it to the hateful and fill their hearts with light
I send it all throughout my day and deep into the night.
I send this love so magical, I beam it all day long
I send this love to God my God for it is my heart song.

Let there be light in all the crevasses of your form, for it longs to illumine the world. It longs to dance and weave across the sky in an effervescent display. It hungers to feed the darkness. It begs to fill and nurture the earth. It wanes and whines to flood all creation with sparks of infinite wonder. Let there be light in all the capillaries of your form. Let it warm your heart as it floods your soul as it illumines your mind and elevates your consciousness. Let the excess pour out on all creation that others may bask in the glow of pure luminosity and feed from its hue.

Let there be light, for love is its sibling, and each need the other to thrive. Light is essential to life, the greater the light, the greater the love. Use your heart and mind to beam light to all creatures great and small.

I call up light the sustenance of body, mind and soul
I call forth light and elevate the world in part and whole.
I call forth light and move all evil that attempts to dwell
I magnify light so intense the darkness it assails.

I raise the light in living things and in the world outside
I raise the light in humankind, the dark I override.
I send forth light to every place where hate pervade and grow
I send forth light to all strangers and everyone I know.

I am the light and it feeds from my soul, my heart, my mind
I am the light and I couple my light, with God I'm aligned.
I am the light and light beams from my hands are quantified
I send great light, by my intent, is this light multiplied.

Light coupled with more light and multiplied with love
Will fill the universe this day and lift all souls thereof.
Light which glistens and dances, I send it to all nations
Light sweet everlasting light, create a light vibration.

"Selflessness is the key to enlightenment.

Love unlocks the door."

I whispered to the winds and my heart was carried through the air,

I whispered to the sky and felt the wings of angels encase my words.

I whispered to the world and saw my intentions being fulfilled,

I whispered to the ancients and saw light engulf the earth.

I whispered, let love reign, let peace flourish, let kindness prevail, let humankind be gentle with each other's hearts, LET THERE BE LOVE and my whispers were felt by all.

"Right now remember you are contagious you are comprised of LOVE, create an epidemic!"

Amazing grace covered me and through the paradigm,

My arms stretched out to love them all, the hateful and the kind.

It was not me I tell you but Spirit in the glow,

It was not of the earthly sod, Divine love overflowed.

I found that in my trials, greater came the light,

I found out from the sages that I was god in God's sight.

I bask in light so magical, I melded in the fold,

Surrendered to the power within, God's face I did behold.

And now the light engulfs me, propels me to convey,

That love is all that matters on any given day.

Be the light, shine your heart, be the love in motion,

LOVE OUTLOUD and spark the flame, create a LOVE commotion.

> *"Clean out your spiritual closet and restock your wardrobe with love."*

There is no better time than now to practice a simple but wonderfully fulfilling ritual. You've heard of a nutritional cleansing, well, I would like you to join me in a spiritual cleansing. It is a simple way to elevate and attune your consciousness and a great way to restore your spirit. It is simpler than you may think and yet the benefits are endless.

Pick the number of days you wish to participate, (I have chosen three weeks) but remember that research has shown, that the neural pathways to developing any new habit require 21 days before that habit becomes automated. Begin with eating fruits, nuts and vegetables and avoid eating red meat which grounds you. During this period of purifying, don't ingest any alcohol and avoid using hairspray or chemicals on your hair such as dyes or mousse. Now comes the hard part, don't judge anyone or anything and minimize your strong opinions or keep them to yourself. Don't curse or use foul language either.

> *"With every foul word you utter another angel leaves your presence."*

Don't condemn, complain or criticize, purify your body and your soul by using an inner and outer dialogue which uplifts you and those around you.

Meditate daily and use the power of the spoken word to pray, sending love to the angels and the Holy Spirit. You will discover that doing all these things feels so good, you will want to do it time and time again. Over the years I have practiced this ritual and not just near or on holidays, but many times when I simply felt so blessed and full of joy, that I wanted to invoke a state of rapture.

A state of rapture is the marriage of quantum love, immense gratitude, overwhelming joy and the indwelling Spirit, in perfect concert with one another. It is a free flow of pure energy, the amplification of your inner child at play in the fields of the Lord. It is ecstasy to the tenth power. It manifests in whatever way you are moved to allow this expansive energy to flow through you, such as dancing, painting, meditating, singing or climbing to the top of a mountain. I am blessed to live near Pikes Peak Mountain, 14,110 feet above sea level and near the Garden of the Gods, which has wonderful trails to hike, places which contribute to feeding the inner light.

I remember years ago when a very famous Academy Award winning actress contacted me and invited me to spend a week with her in Malibu. I was so elated since she had always been one of my favorites and I felt so connected to her that her phone call was, in a metaphoric way, like being invited home. I played the song "Home" from the Broadway production of "The Wiz" over and over again and danced until exhaustion, I was in such a beautiful, blissful rapturous state of joy.

I also remember with intense clarity, December 1, 2006. My girlfriend and I had a powerful meditation that morning and afterward I went about my business as on any normal day. Suddenly at 2:30 in the afternoon, my heart started racing, the energy and frequency in the room suddenly shifted and instantly before me in an effervescent golden, glowing apparition, was an Archangel and in broad daylight too! I was speechless and humbled to my knees. I literally could not speak as this messenger from heaven began blessing my home, waving what looked like a scepter with small drops of water flying about the air. What transpired between us will remain private but I can tell you that I stayed in the silence all day in a quiet, humble state of rapture. All these years later it is still difficult to talk about it, as it was such a powerful heavenly display.

When you make it your intent to live in a state of pure love, when you cleanse your body and pour your heart into passionately purifying your thoughts thus purifying your soul, you will see how elevated your energy and consciousness become. As you eliminate the things which veil you from hearing, seeing or sensing your angels, you raise your own frequency, which enables spiritual vision. You then attract more angels to your life and your dreams begin to show you things that being grounded has prevented. Step up and lend yourself over to a small space in time, when you have a chance to share your pure self with all.

I dreamed beyond a spectrum that others could behold,
I saw things in the distance that they could never know.
My vision was much grander than the naked eye could see,
My heart beheld the future and what was yet to be.

So many fail to look beyond, their minds afraid to soar,
So jaded from the road of life, which left them scarred and torn.
But let not one man kill your hope or take away your dreams,
Keep the spark of hope alive, across the sky trail beams.

For those who dream a grander scale will see beyond the veil,
Extraordinary fields of love which no man can assail.

Ariaa's Ark
All Creatures Great and Small

"All animals add to mother earth's ecosystem. To kill them or to destroy their environment is equivalent to destroying yourself."

I would be remiss if I wrote a book that did not address animals and how vital they are to the earth. It would be unconscionable if I did not attempt to help the masses see the value of each and every animal, insect, and all the creatures of the oceans and seas. Each and every living form of creation adds to the ecosystem and their roles are not only vital but essential.

Animals are my heart and soul. For as long as I can remember I have had pets and loved nature. At three years old while sitting in the woods near my rural home, I found a furry, fun critter and began playing with it. Later that night my right thigh began to swell and grew three times its size. Suffice to say the Tarantula I found that day, had apparently enjoyed me so much, he took a little bite, yet I do not remember feeling him biting me because I was simply having too much fun!

My love for animals has always overridden my common sense. In 1995 while living in Sedona, Arizona, a family of wild boar showed up in my yard at three o'clock in the afternoon. Now anyone knows that if wild animals are out that early foraging for food, they must be pretty hungry since they risk their own lives to be so visible. I tossed some potatoes to them and they scarfed them up so I found a way to ensure they got a good balanced diet. My local grocer was a lovely man who had once been a client of mine. He began giving me sweet potatoes, cabbage, lettuce, apples, pears, carrots and other "damaged" vegetables the store was throwing out. Much to the chagrin of my neighbor across the street, I began feeding the three babies and mama every time they showed up at my door. One morning I was outside with all four boars eating the goodies I had gathered when something suddenly spooked the mom. She ran toward me, meaning me no harm but it caused me to realize that these were indeed very large wild animals and that I needed to be more careful.

In 1997, I was in a ninety-day angelic cycle which as I mentioned before, is when you have a heightened state of awareness and all of your psychic senses are enhanced. You see angels and masters from every culture and you audibly here them, you get profound visions which come to pass as real life events within weeks of seeing them; in essence you are tapped into what we call the "collective conscious" which is a moving hologram where all events past, present and future are known and seen.

Something powerful and memorable happened while I was in this pronounced state of sensory perception. I had just meditated and saw a teeny, tiny spider about the size of a ball point pin head, crawling up the wall and in my effort to save it and free it, something I was not prepared for occurred. I am a firm believer in saving even the tiniest of creatures and I do not kill anything, not even a fly, so it was typically my way to catch the critter with bare hands in order to free it. On this day, as I was attempting to run my finger up under the little guy, I accidently squashed this teeny fellow with my index finger. Running toward the kitchen trying to hurry and wash him off my finger, I suddenly felt a vibration began crawling up my right hand and arm and by the time I got to the kitchen, that energy hit me right in the heart! I instantly knew that I was feeling exactly what that tiny spider felt at the moment of impact when I accidently killed him. I was devastated! I had never killed anything before and could not believe how painful it was for him, but remember there are no accidents. While I used to literally mourn with the passing of squirrels and chipmunks and deer who'd been hit by cars, I have come to learn that when these things happen, it is just as much of a blessing for the animal. It is one of those things you don't see but they move on to their next level of animal consciousness and evolve up the scale of life the same way humans do. Humans have evolved from primitive Neanderthals, to the intelligent, spiritually awakened beings we are today. Animals too move from insect to another form of life, such as perhaps a chipmunk or perhaps a dog or cat. Some animals even make the sacrifice of death, as I feel this one did, to teach and elevate our human conscious awareness, so we grasp how essential their roles are.

> *"The character of a human can be defined by how he treats animals."*

I have such a great respect for nature and I was taught very early on, that every animal responds to love. It is the Universal denominator. The greatest lesson the Sages have taught me is that all creatures, human or animal respond to love. It is the core of every creation and when you raise your own vibration to the higher frequencies of love, compassion and kindness, there is nothing to fear and all will respond in kind to your loving heart. That begs the question, "How does one raise their vibration?" And the answer is very simple and practical. Meditate, heal your emotional issues, discard the emotional baggage, forgive, forget, and affirm all is well. Fake it till you make it, send love to everyone you see, for all is love. Every time you reverse a negative thought or judgment on another, you raise your own vibration. Every time you send love to a crippled man in the store or a dog about to cross the street or a crying child or a stranger you see on the news who has just lost their home or gone through some crisis like a tornado or flood, you raise your own vibration. Every time you pray for a stranger you see, or for those you see on the news each day, every time you lift another, you elevate your own soul. Even if you don't feel particularly loving that day, fake it, send it anyway because the universe is designed like a cosmic boomerang, what you throw out will come right back. You cannot go wrong by sending love and praying for others, because it always comes back to you in one way or another. With every effort you make and practicing all of these actions daily, you will re-attune to the highest frequency in the Universe, love.

I know that I have told you many times but it is worth,
Repeating once again for all the animals of earth.
I watch too many people who mistreat the creatures so,
Mostly due to ignorance or the need to just control.
Ripping out the toenails of a kitten you took in,
Or cutting off the tails of the new puppies is a sin.
You say it's for convenience so the cats don't scratch your stuff,
You say the tails get far too big which in a home can make it tough.

Leaving horses in a field of icy fallen snow,
Walking dogs on hot asphalt is ignorance you know.
Spraying them with chemicals for ticks or fleas is sad,
Ripping them from mom too young is equally as bad.

Muzzling your dog because you're too lazy to train,
Is just as bad as shocking it with that collar, that's insane!
You break the spirit in each one and then you wonder why,
They eat your couch or your screen door it is their way to cry.

"The Story of the Weeping Camel" is a documentary
On how much animals do feel and Mongolians clearly see...
Inside all the souls of those you call the beasts of earth
I beg you pray don't get one if you don't value its worth.

If you take a doggie in and then a few years later
You want to move but not the dog, I urge you reconsider.
Would you give your kid away because it's problematic?
Then see the agony your doggie feels which makes it manic.

People should be screened to see if they are qualified
To really love an animal throughout its entire life.
They feel the same things you do if it hurts you it hurts them
Educate yourself before you take a new pet in.

"Animals contribute to the light mass of earth and should be considered as valuable as any human being."

Animals are just furry people. Don't forget when Moses saved a little lamb he found favor in God's sight. I penned the following as a protest to those who just don't understand the animal world. I know it sounds very harsh, but if we as human beings would be more passionate about protecting nature, if we would take more responsibility in caring for all creatures' great and small, the earth would be more balanced. When it comes to animals, just as I do with people, I try to metaphorically walk in their shoes. If I were a dog, would I like eating the same hard, tasteless food every single day of my life? If I was a cat, would I want my nails ripped out or my testicles cut off or would I want to eat right next to my litter box? If I was a horse, would I want to be left out in a field of snow all winter long with no shelter to protect me from the elements?

I wish more people would try to perceive what an animal feels when they suddenly give it up for adoption because it no longer fits into their life. So many who move to a new state or apartment do just that and I am always saddened to see how traumatized these pets are, who have been so readily cast aside after years of being loyal and loving to their owners. I am horrified when I see someone leave their pet behind where there is a fire looming nearby, instead of taking that baby with them when they evacuate. I am shocked when I see the ignorance of man as they ride their large dogs in an open bed truck at speeds exceeding 50 MPH knowing if anything goes wrong, they are literally making their dog a living projectile! I wrote the following knowing some might be offended and I actually hope it does cause such a rumbling in the stomachs of those who do not think, that they change the way they perceive their pets and all wildlife. Every creature is a gift from God.

You were entrusted with a life but carelessly left the door open and ensured a painful death for your cat as foxes and coyotes ripped it apart.

You were entrusted with a life but you used shock therapy to stiffen the barks of a creature that is designed to bark.

You were entrusted with a life but you left chocolate and Christmas ribbon which is toxic to dogs laying around.

You were entrusted with a life but you rode your dog in the back of your pickup never realizing he would become a living torpedo when you had that fender bender.

You were entrusted with a life but you ripped the finger nails out of your cat because it suited your needs but left that baby traumatized and defenseless if your cat ever had to get away from a predator.

You were entrusted with a life but you feed your cat right next to his toilet, the litter box.

You were entrusted with a life but you left your dog out in the bitter cold with one thin blanket in a drafty shack you call a doghouse.

You were entrusted with a life but you locked your dog in a kennel for long periods of time because you were uninspired to train it.

You were entrusted with a life but you spanked your dog when he had to pee and had no way to get out on his own, as if he was supposed to hold it.

You were entrusted with a life but you left your kids and grandchildren pull its tail and ride on his back.

You were entrusted with a life but you gave your furry baby away when it became inconvenient for you to keep it or when you had to move and didn't make allowances to take your baby with you.

You were entrusted with a life yet you didn't secure the gate when high winds came through and a car found your dog before you could.

You were entrusted with a life..... Do not get a pet if you cannot be responsible enough to ensure its needs are met, that it has food, fresh water, a warm bed, a safe environment and a loving home for the duration of its life.

"Pets are not disposable objects and should not be acquired if you can't keep them for the entire duration of their life".

How can folks give pets away when they have raised them up?
With allergies and excuses which make you want to chuck.
I hear it from the folks I love and from those I don't know
I see it on the TV and it always hurts my soul.

I feel an animal is love and God entrusted it to me
To feed and love and care for 'till his soul has been set free.
I can't imagine ever giving my babies away
I can't imagine how they'd feel if abandoned like a stray.

And yet I see it every day those people who don't see
All animals have feelings, I am sure you can agree.
They were not put upon this earth to endure human strife
If you're going to get one then its best you heal your life.

Heal all those neuroses which can undermine your pet
You pass it on through osmosis then live with the regret.
For when your baby gets disease or sickness look and see
You'll realize you passed it on energetically.

I want to tell you one more story that my dear friends Bill and Betty encouraged me to share with you. For all of you who have lost a beloved pet, perhaps it will give you hope.

Animals, just like humans, reincarnate as they continue up the scale of evolution and growth. Life evolves in every species and animals move from one form to another, repaying karma and learning just as humans do, so what happened in 1999 was of no surprise to me.

I had a little short-haired Chihuahua who was the absolute love of my life. On a winter's night in 1998 he had an attack which was later diagnosed as a tiny spot of cancer on his liver. In a small dog it takes very little to shut them down. Even though it was only a few cancer cells, they had eaten away the lower edge of Kibbles liver.

Michael and I were devastated when Kibbles died in my arms in April of that year but like all animals we assured him, he could come back to our family when he was ready. Typically animals have to stay on the other side long enough to heal whatever physical issue they died of or they return and re-imprint it in the body, just as humans do.

Within less than a year we had moved to Colorado and I began having very strong dreams. In every dream it was the same scenario; I saw Kibbles telling me he was coming back but as a long-haired Chihuahua this time since he never liked the fact, that he was always cold as a short-haired dog. He continued to show me in every dream, that he would be the same color combination of black and camel. I dreamt that Colorado would have an early snowfall in late September and to begin looking for him then.

Weeks went by, then on the twentieth of July, I awoke to this sweet, beautiful aroma filling my bedroom and it was ALL OVER ME! I ran downstairs and said, "Smell me!" to Michael who was making his coffee. He took one sniff and we both charged up the stairs to my bedroom where "new puppy scent" was filling the room! We just stood there smiling because we knew our baby had just been born. We called several pet stores and private breeders that morning and told them to keep an eye out for any new puppies that were black and tan in color and to call me should any arrive.

September rolled around and sure enough, on September 28, 1999, we awoke to two inches of freshly fallen snow. Immediately, we began contacting breeders and looking for our baby. The problem was that we are animal lovers and every puppy is a cute puppy, so I decided to give the heavens a few instructions. I told the angels that I did not want my new puppy traumatized, so I did not want him to ever be caged, nor did I want kids poking at him and scaring him. I also wanted to make sure that I got the right puppy and even though I knew Kibbles' strong personality, I needed something more to ensure we did not take the wrong doggy home. I ask God to make the puppy so cute that it would literally hurt my eyes the very first time that I saw it! Kibbles, was also a very vocal doggy who I had taught to say, "Mama" so I reminded the heavens of that little nugget, just in case all the other criteria failed.

Autumn arrived and we were eagerly ready to take a trip we had planned months earlier with our friends. They were driving from Sedona to meet up at the annual hot air balloon festival in New Mexico. We looked hard to get hotel rooms for us and our doggies, we each had a long haired Chihuahua and we were so looking forward to letting them play together.

Michael had put in a request for vacation months earlier to secure those few days in October, but that did not stop his boss from inexplicably cancelling them at the last minute. I was very sure there was a spiritual reason that we were not intended to leave town.

On the evening we were supposed to travel to New Mexico, I got a call from a woman at a family-owned pet store, who had me on a list to see any new black and tan Chihuahuas. She told me that the puppy she was calling about was supposed to have arrived at their location weeks earlier, but everyone felt he was just too small for it to be safe. Michael had left just hours earlier to go to Canon City for a business meeting. Naturally I called him only to find out that he could not get home in time for us to get to the store before they closed. Calling the store back within minutes, I discovered that the manager had already gone home for the day and when I told her assistant that I was the woman who she had just called about the new puppy, her response surprised me. "Oh well, she took that puppy home because she thought he was too small to leave in a cage overnight!" BINGO! I knew it was my Kibbles.

The next morning we raced to the store before opening time, to meet our little bundle of joy. The manager let us come in and as she closed the large glass doors behind us, I made a request. I told her to please indulge us that I knew this was going to be a little strange, but could she please stand back, open the puppy playpen door while we went to the back of the store where the doggy could not see us. We wanted to see if this little one pound baby could find us. Within seconds the most adorable doggy you have ever laid eyes on, came toddling down the aisle right into my waiting arms! My eyes instantly HURT beyond belief! My heart was so full that I literally thought it would explode! After paying a hefty price which caused Michael's face to contort, we left with our baby in my arms, snug and secure.

I was in euphoric heaven all evening as we played with this tiny little tyke, we fondly named Pokémon when suddenly his body became limp and he stopped breathing! I ran with the puppy in my arms as my husband hurriedly drove the car to the nearest animal emergency center. As we arrived they ran out and took him from me. We sat in the waiting room wondering if we had gotten the wrong doggy and if this was the universe correcting our mistake. To say the least, our spirits were crushed as we waited in agony for the Veterinarian to give us an update.

Within an hour he came out to tell us something odd but logical. Dr. Scott informed us that this little puppy had basically gone into a sugar coma because his liver was underdeveloped. When we looked at the x-ray, Michael and I both became weak at the knees. It could have easily been Kibbles x-ray since the part of Pokémon's liver which was "underdeveloped" was identical to where the cancer had eaten away at Kibbles liver a year and a half earlier. The door to the lobby opened and this little one pound bundle of joy ran right over to me. The doctor inquired, "How long have you had this puppy?" I replied, "About six hours." He remarked, "That is unbelievable and pretty rare for a puppy to be so alert and so bonded with its owner so quickly." But we knew the truth.

The next night I was on the phone with my best friend, sitting in my Lazy Boy rocker, with my feet up and my darling Pokémon sleeping in my lap. The front door opened, Michael arriving home from work and the sound startled Pokémon! With my friend on the phone and Michael standing there, Pokémon exclaimed, "Mama Mama!" All three of us screamed almost simultaneously, "It really is KIBBLES!!!"

Pokémon gave me the best thirteen years I have ever known. He sang with me on every song, was joyful and such an easy baby to love. I knew a lot about animals and caring for them, but I tell you truly, that Pokémon was so human that it was easy to treat him like one. There was not a single day that he did not delight my spirit and fill my heart with everlasting joy. He crossed over the rainbow bridge seven days after his thirteenth birthday in the wee hours of the morning of July 27, 2012. He died in my arms just thirteen days after my beloved fifteen year old cat Tweetums died, also in my arms.

Our animals are just like our family members, they too return to us and are guided back by our familiar vibrations and energy. The loss of a pet is one of the most excruciating heartaches a human endures, so it is a comfort to know, that many times they will see you again, when they return to your family in another form.

Psalms from the Soul

Parables for Conscious Living

Before this book was even conceived, I was penning "Ariaaisms~ Spiritual Food for the Soul" and emailing them to friends and clients. Originally they were poems I referred to as lessons or tidbits of consciousness in rhythmic form. I was searching for a digestible way to convey basic truth principles but wanted to do it in a very light-hearted way as I have been known to be rather intense when I am teaching. One morning, I awoke and words flooded my mind and poured from my soul. With every verse, the words compounded the infinite well of wisdom I had been privy to throughout my spiritual walk. Sages from all walks of life had administered to my soul and now in rhymes and messages, they conveyed the teachings all over again, but this time it was for the masses to read.

Over the years, these scribblings have been synopsized and reworded to fit into social media formats and have become entertainment for those who are searching, but aren't really interested in evolving. When I began writing and compiling this book I felt it would be a nice way to sum up all I have penned here, so I have chosen several of my favorite social media posts. In this chapter and in the following chapter, you will find some of my original Ariaaisms.

Read them as a daily devotional or affirmations to inspire you whenever you need an uplifting word or whenever you are feeling a bit more introspective. I am prayerful they will resonate with you and impart some wisdom in a beautiful, digestible way which feeds your soul.

Take to flight it's time to soar beyond the great divide,

Raise your consciousness and share the gifts you hold inside.

Leave a mark of goodness on everything you do,

Love with all your heart and soul, the everlasting hue.

The universe is full of that which human eyes can't see,

With colors that you know not, it's no hyperbole.

Expand your heart, extend your mind, behold the color hues,

The greatest master lives and breathes right inside of you.

The light of day has ceased to glow and night embraces dark,

I contemplate this day to see, where I left a spark.

Did I touch a heart, a mind, did I lead with LOVE,

Did I make a difference to those here or above?

Then angels whisper, say goodnight and so I take my leave,

But I'll return when morning breaks to plant another seed.

Angels whispered to me but my ears refused to hear,

Silence followed me but my feet ran faster still.

Light beckoned unto me but its fire was all consuming,

Love bathed me in its light but I hid as it was looming.

Then the voices whispered, "I will teach you how to fly",

Instantly my feet left earth and I soared throughout the sky.

Bask in the glow of mornings light let genesis unfold;

Renew your soul by letting go of that which veils your soul.

Release those habits negative, release what does not serve,

Rise from the ashes and embrace the love that you deserve.

For genesis begins within, where Divine LOVE is found,

Discover all the gifts within, another morning coming down.

I am my brother's keeper; he hurts, I hurt, he hungers, I hunger.

I am my sister's keeper; I feel her sorrow in my soul, I sense her joy across thousands of miles.

I take care of you and good karma takes care of me.

I am humankind, kind built right in.

I am the same composition of every living being.

I am energy in mass.

In the remembrance of who I am, I remember who we all are.

I poured out love upon mankind and blazed a trail of passion,

I emphasized that love entails a heart full of compassion.

I held a vision strong and pure that everyone would see,

That they are gods and one with God,

It's up to you and me.

We must use our hearts and minds to alter life's terrain,

We must hold the vision to eliminate world pain.

Knowing is the element which moves through time and space,

Love is the ingredient which cures the human race.

Align yourself to what is good, to what is kind and pure,

Raise your consciousness and find the entire world is cured.

Shades of light, cast great streams, on doors closed long ago,

A genesis, to measure faith, and hope within the soul.

I ponder all the miracles many do not see,

I give praise for a heart on fire and what is yet to be.

There are no limits, there are no bounds, if you just surrender,

To all the power that lies within, if each of you remember,

That deep in you there is a well, a river full of blessings,

Anything is possible, when love you are expressing.

The winds of change are blowing, it is wise to just let go,
Rise above the drowning tide, surrender to the flow.

For what you cling to you shall lose, the light must dance and glean,
Freedom comes in letting go, create a peaceful scene.

An open heart, an open mind, pulsations from above,
Will guide your path; illuminate, the heart that's full of love.

Winding through the paradigms which dance and then collide,
Transformation comes to those who swallow hollow pride.

Bend the way the road turns, be flexible each day,
You never know what angels bring, so get out of their way.

Time begins to settle in imprinting a lifetime of the souls' earthly walk, now seared into the flesh. I could color my hair but each silver strand represents someone that I loved and worried or prayed for. I could see a plastic surgeon but each wrinkle reflects times of hardship and struggle; each and every sign of time upon my face represents the conquests, the accomplishments, and the mastery of it all. And everywhere gravity sets in, my soul has been humbled and seasoned by the toll time is taking. With each new lump, with every jiggle of my body, with every gray hair and every wrinkle which kisses my face, I am reminded of a life well spent, of hardships overcome, wisdom gained, and mountains moved. A soul in flight does not change the terrain for the terrain changes you and when the land grows devoid of green pastures, you feed from golden fields of grain until it's time to soar.

Awaken to the world you paint with your thoughts every day. There are no victims only those unaware of their karma, past or present, those blind to what they have attracted, good or bad; those who fail to take personal responsibility and discover the blessings within each life event. Change your perceptions by discovering yourself, go within, meditate, seek the higher wisdom, which lies within every soul. Seek the higher solutions which come in the silence where angels and sages eagerly await to help you overcome and master all you came to earth to fulfill. Wake up, tune in, spiritually evolve and stop blaming your family, your friends and the world for the lot you have drawn into your life. With every hardship there is mastery awaiting to be engaged. With every heartache overcome, the soul quantum leaps. With every negative event, a positive one is sure to follow. The earth is built on opposite polarities thus, what goes up will come down, what comes down will rise again. There is a purpose and a reason unto all things. Seek to understand the measure of what you are creating, what you are a magnet to and learn to create with greater strokes of the paintbrush of life. For those who seek create the art of mastery, know thyself and discover the paradisiacal within.

There was a time when men and women shared the same values. They worked toward the same goal, they valued honesty, loyalty and relied upon each other. They built the dream together. There was a time when what was important was worth making an effort for, when you would go out of your way to ensure success in that which mattered. There was a time when the goal led to cooperation and a spirit of understanding that in the end, they would be better for having shared the dream. Today's society is disposable. Everything and everyone disposable, replaceable and while that may work with things and stuff, it is not the way humankind was created and it is not the way humankind will thrive. People need people to learn from, to teach, to share, to grow, to inspire, to be a shoulder in times of pain, to be a tower of strength in times of travail. To be there in the end when the days of youth leave your face and the clouds grow grayer from the passage of time. Whether it is a friend, a spouse, a husband, a wife, a lover, a sister, a brother or a kind neighbor, the bottom line is that no one wants to die alone, to be forgotten to be disposed of. You are an original, you are not replaceable in any area of life or love. Value you and the rest of the world will, too. Plan a life that includes each other for you will be the richer for it in the end and so will those who choose to take that walk with you. No one is disposable; all are a gift to life.

We may look differently and think differently, we may be exact opposite polarities; we may be passionate about our ideology, our philosophy, our politics, and our vision, but in the end cut us with the same blade and the majority of us will bleed. When human beings finally grasp the basic concept that to hurt one is to hurt all, when we finally understand the elementary principle that LOVE and civility cultivated en'masse will produce greater and more effective results than its

counterpart; when we finally act from a spirit of oneness and exercise a gentler dialogue, when light is included as partner to reason, when we understand that division makes a weak nation, battle is the food of ignorant fools and feeds the darkness, when we finally awaken spiritually as a whole there will be real change.

"The Song of One"

You can be rich, poor, full-figured, skinny, white, black, or purple with pink polka-dots. You can be straight, gay, transgender, bi-sexual, atheist, agnostic, religious or spiritual, Democrat, Republican, Libertarian or Independent. You can be alone or in a relationship or married and still be lonely. Loneliness does not care if you love yourself or don't, it does not discern whether you are pretty or average looking. It doesn't even care whether you were raised in a good family with love and support or on the streets with nothing. Loneliness finds every human being at one time or another and is different than being alone. Many people are lonely and unless you are looking, you won't see it. You can live alone and be quite content with yourself enough to recognize that being alone is preferred to being with the wrong people but alone does not constitute lonely. Loneliness is often a moment in time, a passing emotion which fades with the dawn and is often magnified with age. The older we get the more we as humans seem to succumb to its reaches.

What are the antidotes to loneliness? Sometimes you just have to feel it and take from it whatever wisdom you can expunge to heal the child within. But other times you can use it as a catalyst to reach out to those in nursing homes, those on the streets, those in shelters or simply the old lady in the grocery store with the hollow stare in her eyes, as she walks aimlessly through the market. Befriend her and those who spend holidays alone, so many more do than you may realize. Spend time in animal shelters or in the children's wing of a hospital and don't forget to take some treats, even if it's just a small stuffed animal for a child or bedding for an animal.

Alone does not have to mean lonely. There are 99.6 million people over 18 who are single in America; that's 44% of the population. For every 100 unmarried women, there are 88 unmarried men and many come with scars too deep to couple in a healthy relationship.

Most of us would prefer our own company to the company of the wrong person. Many of us don't have family, or what family we have, we prefer not to intertwine with. Many of us have lost our loved ones or mates to death and some have simply never found the person they want to share their life with. Whatever the case, it is clear that many are spending more and more time alone.

Social media is the new lonely hearts club and has given many a way to create a new kind of family. But the real key is be comfortable in your own skin and to take this "alone time" to a new level of going deeper within.

You have an opportunity to embrace new challenges, try new experiences, learn new skills or just learn about yourself. You can spiritually evolve through meditation and heal what needs to be healed in those moments when alone becomes lonely.

Instead of pining over what might have been or having a pity party, why not embrace how wonderful it is to have the freedom to explore yourself and discover what makes you tick. Why not celebrate the time you have to yourself, nap, and give the angels a chance to work on you. Discover what makes you laugh, find what makes you wiser, or what makes you feel good about yourself. Read, travel, journal, cook, dance, take a class or two, volunteer your time, help someone in need, exercise, meditate or just sit on the porch and watch the sunset.

Use your loneliness to give of yourself to others, to reach out and touch the life of someone else. Not only does that warm feeling of helping another fill you up, but you will find in serving others your own emptiness is suddenly transformed and with the giving of love, loneliness transmutes to joy. Take a look at how you perceive being alone and realize what a gift it is, especially when you recognize that you now have the angels and Spirit, as a captive audience.

"The Imprint You Leave Behind"

"I may not pass this way again therefore let me leave love laden along the road."

After my clinical death in the Alps of Austria in 1993, I saw the world in an entirely different light. I remember seeing people who had just crossed over, particularly the ones that died at their own hand from suicide and I was astounded at the numbers who killed themselves over a paltry sum of money. To someone who has babies to feed, a mortgage to pay and health issues, I am sure $3,000.00 seemed like an insurmountable amount, but when you think about it, that is a very small price for a life.

I also remember seeing some elderly folks who died and was amazed at how few had planned for their demise. So many left all the details of their funerals, celebrations of life, the decisions of what to do with their homes and stuff, everything had been left to whomever was willing to deal with it and folks having been there myself, that is a lot of stress to leave to someone you love.

The souls that had prepared and left instructions behind for their families and friends seem to be at the greatest level of peace as they transitioned. As I watched souls arrive, no matter how rich or how poor, how old or not so old, no matter how successful or unsuccessful, the majority had one thing in common which completely dumbfounded me. None of those I saw arriving were the least bit concerned about the legacy they had left behind. Not one.

"The love you give while on the earth lives on long after you leave it."

Leaving a legacy is as important as life itself, for what will your life have amounted to if you leave nothing useful behind? We share the planet with seven billion people and approximately one-fourth actually leave something useful behind when they leave this earth. Whether is it an invention, product, literature, movies, poetry, art, music, dance, philosophy, or something else, you have to wonder what the world would be today if everything every soul did while on the earth, vanished with them when they died. Every person has a divine role to play and yet navigates the terrain oblivious to the importance of the dance. Every movement is synchronized to the rhythms of perfect love, like a child in the universal womb, every action births a ripple, every grace-filled step becomes earth's architecture, and every thought creates reality. With every pirouette the dance intertwines with the ballet of all creation. The rogue steps taken outside of the nurturing womb of divine love generate waves of indifference and leaves holes in the fabric of all creation.

For whatever reason, leaving something useful behind is very important to me. I want to know that when I die, my quotes and poetry which have inspired millions will continue to inspire generations to come. I want to know that the music I've recorded will still sing in the hearts of those who resonated with my voice and perhaps they will even be able to "feel" me and all the love I pour into my songs, at the moment they play it. I want to know that the animal rights I have fought for has made a difference for animals of the future, that the oceans and mountaintops I have fought to keep clean will be a pleasing place for those who navigate their terrain and waters years from now. I want to believe that harp seals will never have to endure being brutally bludgeoned by men too cruel to think about, that white Bengal tigers, gorillas, elephants and rhinoceros will roam freely in multitudes, safe and protected. It is my sincere hope that the countless years and hours I have spent elevating the consciousness of groups and individuals and their offspring will bear fruit, and that those who embraced the teachings and principles I have taught, will live and thrive in harmony with all creation for eons to come. It is my ardent belief that by holding the light, by beaming love, light and joyous laughter to all humanity every single day for more than twenty-five years, that it will continue to multiply and manifest as unconditional love, respect for life, great compassion for all and eternal wisdom will be birthed in the hearts of every living soul; that one day, not too far in the future, the combination of these will seed the tree of peace for all humankind.

Are you living with intention or are you simply taking up space on the planet? Are you creating anything which will be useful to those you love or perfect strangers when your body no longer draws breath? Are you making a difference each day, even if only to those you love? Do you have some unique gift that you are withholding because you lack vision, motivation, or the time to bring it to fruition? There is no time like the present to generate and share all the gifts you hold inside. Imagine what the world would be if everyone without exception, left a meaningful legacy behind.

"Your flight depends on your willingness to soar with the change of the winds, on your commitment to complete the flight and on your courage to charter territories unknown. Your wings can only carry you as far as your mind allows."

I have had pets all my life and for the past 30 years all of them have lived to be old aged and all have died in my arms including my two eldest, who recently died just 13 days apart. It occurred to me how many people don't really know how to handle death. Not just of animals but of humans too. We often fail to remember that death is a natural part of life and it is only fear, ego and selfishness that gets in the way of the natural process unfolding. I am fortunate enough to live what I teach which is all about emotional balance, spiritual faith and surrendering and letting go. Instead of clinging or trying to control the process, I simply pour LOVE and cuddle the one dying. Instead of trying to cling, I call in the Archangels, angels and a host of nameless faceless others who work in the fields of the Lord to facilitate such matters. We often forget that it is in clinging that you create a space of suffering, it is in trying to control death or push it away that struggle occurs. Death is inevitable but how you respond to it can be the difference in whether the soul leaving the earth experiences a peaceful crossing or one full of pain, suffering and struggle. Selflessness is the key....you can grieve after they've gone but until then be thoughtful of the person or animal you love and help it make the transition by being as loving and selfless as you can. Hold them, cuddle them, kiss them, and thank them for all they have added to your life...then let them soar.

"Mother Earth is sacred and you are just her guest."

She is warming, she is melting, she is languishing and needs your loving care. There are places you don't see and never will if you turn a blind eye to nature. There are medicinal gifts she is waiting to show you in rainforests you will never know, if you cut down the trees of life. There are mysteries awaiting in the oceans, ones that add to you wisdom and ones which feed history but you may never drink from that knowledge if you pollute her waters. Mother Earth weeps for you, mankind, and cries out, "They know not what they do, yet they know and choose to turn away". The height of arrogance and ignorance is to know yet do nothing.

Poetic Rhythms for the Dance of Life

"I cannot explain the odd happenings of my heart but love pours from it like crystal warm waters drenching all those in my path"

It is said that when words flow in rhymes and lilting rhythms from the lips of a human being, it is because the angels are speaking through them. The many mansion worlds, also known as heaven, hold mysteries and doors which you can only enter once you have left the earth and arrived at the gates. A few of us have had the sheer honor and pleasure of being given a glimpse and insight into these kingdoms while on our journey of transcendent love. There are colors beyond the spectrum you have on earth; there are spider-like webs of mathematical codes which are assigned to every living form of creation; there are star formations which lend themselves to certain skills and strengths, which many know on earth as a diluted form of astrology. There is a heavenly choir where music is an orchestrational continuum and there are prisms of light which form holograms, where everything every human being has said, thought or done is a never-ending, recorded motion picture, replaying every event, every lifetime and every moment in time. And there are hosts and legions of angelic hierarchy who assist, guide and keep the infinite wisdom of the Creator activated and alive.

The Archangel Raphael has been with me from the beginning, since I experienced my transformation in Austria in 1993. Raphael is the angel of music, poetry and the arts which suits me beautifully since my birth sign is Taurus, which governs all of those elements. I am certain that his presence in my life lends to some of the words which seemingly flow from my lips.

The following are just a few of the thousands of poetic parables which have come to me over the past few years and each one contains its own message of hope, inspiration, aspirations, and ideals. As you read them, breathe them in. Let the words consume you for in the moment you look upon some of these words, an angel will join you. They enjoy humans as much as we enjoy them and they delight in all transformations, but especially those which arrive through poetry, verse, music and the arts.

Wikipedia describes a virtue as "Moral excellence. A virtue is a positive trait or quality deemed to be morally good and thus is valued as a foundation of principle and good moral being. Personal virtues are characteristics valued as promoting collective and individual greatness."

These poetic principles or spiritual virtues are spackled throughout the book to punctuate the relevance of living a harmonious life. All these are essential to maintaining balance and when implemented, are the foundations to sustaining well-being. The virtues we have already addressed in this book are:

- Laughter
- Emotional balance
- Courtesy
- Dependability
- Integrity
- Discipline
- Self-love

- Self-respect
- Self-expression
- Honor
- Connecting to nature
- Connectivity to the animal kingdom
- Listening
- Forgiveness
- Intention
- Generosity
- Loyalty
- Patience
- Compassion
- Purity

I've selected a few other virtues for this chapter which complete the foundation of a walk in harmony with all creation.

- Selflessness
- Body
- Mind
- Soul
- Kindness
- Sanctuary
- Self-Discovery
- Diversity
- Manifestation
- Gratitude
- Karma

- Surrender
- Humility
- Character
- Judgment
- Discernment

Being virtuous is not about being a saint. These ideals are simply the basis to generate harmony in the life of a human being. However, when practiced even occasionally, these spiritual virtues will free you from the constraints of worldly cares and elevate your light, thus elevating your communication with angels and the Divine.

Selflessness

"Doing something nice for another has lasting effects on your own soul"

What did you do on this day, with whom did you connect?
Did you lend a helping hand, show others some respect?
Did you leave your mark on someone's heart, what did you do?
Did you smile at a stranger or a neighbor who was new?

Did you pay the tab for someone running short of change?
Did you help them with their load as they tarried in the rain?
Did you compliment someone who looked like they were lost?
Did you pause to help someone without first weighing the cost?

Perform an act of selflessness and do it often please
There's more to life than self-pursuits and getting what you need.
There's humanity at work each day so read between the lines
Anticipate the greater need, give of yourself and time.

The acts of kindness ever small can leave a lasting mark
You'll never know what others think and what your acts impart.
But from my own experience I'm told it means so much

To those who don't expect it to come from a strangers' touch.

Take the time to reach and touch and uplift humankind
Take the time to bond with souls and become intertwined.
For when you leave this planet the thing you miss the most
Is humans and all that they bring you can't feel as a ghost.

"Love without an agenda encases energy so proportionate to God that it permeates the universe and leaves a mark on everything it touches."

Love which knows no boundaries, the unconditional kind
Is timeless and is priceless and often a rare find.
So many people think that they are masters at this realm
I tell you if you test that love their love will often fail.

For love which knows no boundaries, resolute and unrequited
Is love of such pure measure all the heavens are united.
Let me attempt to define it, this love all absolute
Allow me to cast my gaze toward the effervescent hue.

I speak of love deliciously abounding without doubt
Free-flowing from a sacred well that's never known a drought.
I speak of sparks that light the air like fireflies in June
I live to tell that's how I feel, when with God I commune.

It translates not to human words or love which passes through
It transcends all emotions to the very depths of you.
It goes beyond the greater spectrum which gratifies your soul
The love I speak of is complete and in it you're made whole.

It permeates your beingness with such a warm embrace
It lights your world, your everything, you wear it on your face.
It reaches far beyond you to expand to others so
They don't know why the feel so good when you come and go.

It's visible yet not I tell you for you seek nothing
This love is lasting and prevails beyond all human things.
Wear this love by reaching deep inside yourself today
Just send love to everyone you pass along the way.

Send it out whether or not your feel it, for it comes
Fake it till you make it folks, God's greater work is done.
You will see how love lifts you when you're the instrument
You will each know love greater by all that you have sent.

***Today remember that selflessness is the key to enlightenment.
Love unlocks the door.***

*"Prayer is your direct line to the invisible
to create the visible."*

Pray whenever you're in need and find within that hour,
The awe- inspiring manifold that comes from prayer power.

Pray for those you'll never meet, search for souls to raise
Pray for anything you want then seal it with your praise.
Pray for others every day, your soul is covered too
For everything you wish for them, comes right back to you.

Pray for all world leaders and those who won't make peace
Pray for those you're fond of and those called enemies.
Pray for all the elderly and those who are alone
Prayer is communiqué into the worlds unknown.

Pray when you have heartaches, for the "Comforter" appears
Pray when you need someone and God will dry your tears.
Pray when you are hungry and manna fills you full
Pray when you need nothing...an unknown golden rule.

Pray with great intensity and answers will come forth
Pray with little effort and that is all it's worth.
Pray for all the animals who wander in the road

Pray that they're protected and our God will make it so.

Pray for all the angels for they need prayers too
Lift your voice and thank them for always helping you.
Pray for God to lead you and guide you through your day
Pray for God to send you someone wise to light the way.

Please pray softly, pray aloud, make time to let God know
Pray with others or alone, for what you reap, you sow.
Pray for what is visible and what you cannot see,
I am praying for you right now, I hope you'll pray for me.

Today may you experience the ultimate communion that comes from praying.

Body

"Retreat, reflect, recharge and the results will be renewal and restoration."

Find a place to rest your head and rest your heart there too,
Find a place to call your own like all great masters do.
Seek to be alone with self and with the God within,
Seek to be in solitude where you can heal and mend.

A sacred well within you will rise up with waters pure,
The thoughts you leave outside the door will vacate you for sure.
Bring your soul back to the center where love thrives so great,
Bring your heart straight to the throne, shadows eliminate.

For life is at times massive as the world spins fast and queer,
And life can be so daunting when your own voice you can't hear.
Retreating to a place where you can rest and be at peace,
Will bring you sweet renewal as your shadows you release.

The Light can feed you energy which empowers all your cells,
You can reflect on what your purpose is and what compels.
You'll come to see yourself the way they view you from above,
You'll come to view yourself as an extension of Gods' love.

"The body is a temple of the Living God. How you adorn it is a direct reflection of the God that lives within you."

When you step outside your house, what do others view?
Is your hair an uncombed mess, is this the best of you?
Do you ever stop to think, the image you project
Sends a message about the God you worship and respect?

For you are God internally and what the outside shows,
Is indicative of Light, the Light of God, it glows.
You are a walking billboard of how great Creator is,
You determine what other's see, down-trodden or pure bliss.

Think about the souls who dress their bodies without thought
Would you want to serve the God that shows in what they've got?
You can have no money and still be neatly dressed
You can be as rich as Trump and still look quite the mess.

How are you cloaked daily, are you neatly tucked and groomed?
Money doesn't matter here but that you are attuned.
Attuned to care about yourself and what the world will see
Do others want to know the God inside of you and me?
If they don't then take a look and find a way to shine
For you are a reflection of our God, the great Divine.

"Transmitting energy is easier than you may think…transmit, transmute and transformation will occur"

Did you know your hands are made for more than realized?
Did you know their usefulness is heavens great surprise?
Light so quantified can stream from both of your hands
You can become the instrument of God, the great I AM.

You simply need enfold yourself in the Golden Light within
To have not an agenda causes beams to flow and send.
Beam love of high proportion to the object waiting there…
A heart, a knee, a shoulder or to someone in despair.

You are amplifications of a Creator God so great
Your hands will heat like morning sun and instantly pulsate.
With light beams you can fill the world beyond your understanding
For beams will permeate the air and continue on expanding.

Your prayers tumble from your lips and take a joyful ride
On a beam of light they go, through the universe they glide.
They land on ears of angels with their love intensely bright
They're answered and returned to you on another beam of light.

It's the constant of the universe to work in ethers there
Using all God's energy at your disposal and in your care.
You must expand your world today and do what masters do
Use your hands as instruments and let God's light shine through.

Mind

"Discipline of the mind ignites rapture of the soul"

Your mind is what you make it though it is a great machine
Enhanced by wisdom and of course by having self-esteem.
A proficient mechanism to nurture and retrain
What you feed it will soon grow in the connectors of the brain.

It behooves the soul to feed it love and to feed it great teachings
It behooves the soul to sing and pray and offering great blessings.
It behooves the soul to dance with joy and to read a book each week
It behooves the soul to heal the things which cause the brain to peak.

Affirmations are a good way to calm with peaceful flow
Meditation is another way to fine tune as you go.
Prayer is a grand way to facilitate the best
Train your brain to be at peace and to release the stress.

The light of God cannot come through a rampant moving target
If your brain is acting out you are off the spiritual market.
You have dominion that's a fact over mind and body too
Take a nap in the afternoon to enhance the best in you.

Rapture soon will find you in extraordinary ways
If you still the body and you flat line the brain waves.
The highest light will join you in an effervescent glow
Be still and get in touch with God and elevate your soul.

Soul

"Tend to the garden of self-improvement every day and your soil will grow fertile"

Shine me God and polish me to glisten like the sun
Shine me God and as I extend your love to everyone
Shine me God and help me be the grander child you made
Shine me Lord and let me lift each person every day.

Build me God a stronger frame that I may walk for years
Build my shoulders broader Lord for others falling tears.
Build me God a softer voice to pray for those who hate
Build me nonjudgmental Lord before it gets too late.

Grow me God a vessel which you place your gifts within
Grow me God more wisdom so your gifts I can extend.
Grow me God an instrument of healing light this day
Grow me a peacemaker, its peace for all I pray.

*"Souls often collide in unawake remembrance
of yesterdays gone by"*

Have you ever met someone who heightened all your thoughts?
Have you lost your balance in remembering what once was?
Souls collide so many times and yet so unaware
The feelings that they're feeling lead to other lifetimes shared.

Your life today is connected by the karma that you made
Your life is so much more than the plans you think you laid.
Your life is joined, encircled by the souls you knew before
Your life is meant to reconnect to open up new doors.

Emerged in sweet remembrance which comes in dreams each night
You'll see all those in your life now add to your own sweet light.
But if you find in memories that pain comes back again
Perhaps it's best to shield yourself and just remain good friends.

For love and life and past lives too are fragile and need molding
You decide how much to heal the emotions that you're holding.
You decide what's best for you as you soar upon your way
You choose who to nurture and who to send away.

Today remember that everyone in your life today with rare exception you have known in other lifetimes. It is up to you to determine the reason they are back and what can be learned or derived.

Kindness

"Common courtesy is the front door to inviting angels in and opens new worlds when extended to human beings". A thank you goes a very long way.

Long ago in days gone by, good manners were expected,
The social grace of families therein clearly reflected.

Politeness was a ticket into horizons unexplored,
An invitation to the ball, where you wouldn't be ignored.

When gentlemen were chivalrous and ladies oh so prim,
A please and thank you was what you extended to the brim.

Today we barely speak aloud to people passing by,
We briefly smile and never look each other in the eye.

We fail to give a wave in traffic when we are let in,
We fail to write a thank you note to a very thoughtful friend.

Most children are not shown the ways of thoughtfulness, it's true,
Most children learn from watching just exactly what you do.

Adults are the example for a world that's yet to be,
Are you teaching anyone about common courtesy?

Are you the exception on this earth, the one who lights and shines,
Are you the thoughtful being who is genuine and kind?

Do you think of others for no reason but to be,
The one who gives a loving call to check upon their needs?

Do you send a thoughtful card or let them know you care,
People are a fragile lot, they need to know you're there.

Today awaken to the fact that you can make a difference,
It's all about the thoughtfulness and not just the appearance.

Today remember that the smallest courtesy could be the one which grants you the keys to heaven. You never know what form an angel on earth will take.

"There is no greater compliment than that which comes from showing genuine interest in a complete stranger"

Listen, are you listening, I have so much to say
While traveling I meet so many people every day.
I find that I care deeply about their daily tasks
I find folks oh so interesting and grow friendships that will last.

I see some folks around me and they just don't seem to care
About their fellow beings who are passing here and there.
But life is about growing and if you'll take a look
Every person that you meet is a fascinating book.

You'll hear them tell of journeys and the hardships that they've faced
You'll hear them speak of miracles and how they found God's grace.
You'll hear them telepathically their faces reveal much
You'll have the chance to make them laugh, a life that you can touch.

You'll hear them whisper sweetness and the lot they feel from you
You'll see that you're the instrument God's light is shining through.
You'll find a warm embrace from each will compliment your soul
You'll see we're all connected in the greater cosmic whole.

I learn so much by hearing what my fellow humans speak
I learn so much from faces when I find them shy and meek.
I learn so much from hugging for a hug speaks volumes too
I learn to love them everyone for like me, they're gods too.

Today sit up and take a genuine interest in a fellow human being…it may just be an archangel you are entertaining.

Sanctuary

"Your home should be a sacred haven which reflects the light within you."

Have you walked into a home where everything was dreary?
The color scheme and darkened rooms screamed of down and weary?
Your home should be a lovely space reflecting your own light,
The décor should speak volumes to your senses, to your sight.

A home should be more than a place you hang your hat and coat,
Filled with warmth, inviting scents, the sacred to denote.
A sacred sanctuary filled with love and beauty too,
Inviting to the eyes and heart, a reflection of you.

It matters not what kind of things you choose to fill your space,
What matters is the way you feel while in your sacred place.
A home can be made beautiful for your aura is the key,
Just fill your home with love, joy, light and let God take the lead.

Today remember there's no place like home…make it special.

Self-Discovery

Triggered by a memory I traveled far to find…
The very remnants of myself, encapsulated there in time.
You see the soul knows boundaries not and does not seek to stall
The spirit works in each of us to gently heal the flaws.

Like a microcosm in each cell there dwells a tale
From the lives you've lived before on land and seas you sailed.
All the actions, all the deeds and all the feelings too
Are written in the Book of Life and written there in you.

As you grow in Spirit and awaken all these ghosts
You'll find that you will travel to the places you loved most.
In dreams and meditation will the universe reveal…
All that caused you hurt or pain so that you may be healed.

Once you see where you have roamed and what you did before
You'll find that you are so empowered to open greater doors.
The more doors that you open and the more you come to know…
The more you reach enlightenment by healing all the old.

Diversity

"Travel opens up new worlds of observation, learning and embracing the diversity of humankind."

How wonderful to be home from a trip across the globe
How wonderful to meet so many folks I did not know.
How wonderful to walk the steps where others use to dwell
How wonderful to hear the stories perfect strangers tell.

When you see the world at large you find that it is so
We're all so very much alike in what we love and hold.
The struggle just in weather as the rain beats down on those...
Who rush to catch the morning train sipping coffee in wet clothes.

The Britons are a quiet lot who do not wish to chatter
The Scots were full of words to speak their clothes a bit more tattered.
The Irish were so proper and so lovely in their speech
The world is full of beauty in the people that you meet.

I walked on streets where Rob Roy roamed, where Kings and Queens have been
I bask in sunlit streets of brick inside a state of Zen.
I ate with all the finery of Aristocrats at play
I shopped at Harrods happily for more than half a day.

And in an old cathedral built a thousand years ago
I communed in sweet surrender meditating in the fold.
Visions came in multitude cascading in my view
My energy ten times increased my spirit so renewed.

Drink in unique venues to enhance your spirit and feed your mind and body through the hospitality of other nations.

I've met so many people as my days of life flow by,
Some so good right to the bone it makes you want to cry.
I've met some with great character and some with none at all,
I've met some who are always there and some who never call.

I've met some souls who trouble me, their childlike thoughts repeat,
I've met some who hold on to pain and wallow in defeat.
I've met some who are powerful and those who think they are,
I've met some who are ignorant and some who shine like stars.

I've met some who are players and treat women oh so wrong,
I've met some who are lonely for someone's love they long.
I've met some who say nice things and some who hate so loud,
I've met some with integrity who rise above the crowd.

I've met some who just baffle me inconsistent in their ways,
I've met those who befriend you and yet they still betray.
I've met my share of rock stars of divas and of fools,
I've met my share of angels, those who live outside the rules.

I've met so many people, who delight my spirit so,

I've met so many lights of God it simply makes me glow.

I've met some in other countries, who make my heart skip beats,

I've met some in my travels, some I'd like to keep.

The world is full of people how much they light me up.

The world is such a smorgasbord, drink from the people cup!

"Travel enriches the soul and leads to the most fascinating discoveries."

Appreciate the places where so many people roam
Those that can be found abroad and those right here at home.
Every country has its own, a beauty which shines through
Like all the people in the world, just like me and you.

I've wander through grand fields of green in Austria my land
I've walked the streets of Paris, Germany the Fatherland.
I viewed the North Sea in the spring where Vikings use to sail
I walked the halls of castles where great kings and queens prevailed.

I've prayed in old cathedrals where the Spirit of God thrives
I've been consumed by ancient lands, gained knowledge as the prize.
I've been so blessed to love them all, those far away and near
I've met the finest people who have touched my heart so dear.

I urge you to open your hearts to other worlds of gold
I urge you all to travel and fulfill your very soul.
There's more to life you can embrace by walking in the shoes
Of those in other countries with so many different views.

Life is too short to travel in a world of ordinary
Life is meant to be meaningful and so extraordinary.
So many people here to love and yet so little time
Reach out and touch them one by one, love leads to the Divine.

Today remember to expand your knowledge, extend yourself and explore this most beautiful of all planets.

Manifestation

"Whatsoever you wish for, whatsoever you call forth, has already been given you by the measure of your faith."

What is it that you wish for, do you pray for it at night?
What is it that you hold near, dream of with all your might?
Whatsoever you hold in heart and in the silence too
Whatsoever you believe becomes your highest truth.

You see the mind is the machine connected to the soul
The trigger which creates the wish is that you have to know.
You have to know with all your heart and believe with all your mind
That what you wish is given you as gift from the Divine.

If you want to move that mount then write a letter out
Show all of your intentions and that you have no doubt.
Do you want a soul mate is that your desire
Anything you wish to have, with love you can acquire.

Use some affirmations and visualize the best
Pray and give some thanks up and faith will do the rest.
Faith is more than believing, it's knowing that it's done

With knowing there's assurance that what you dream will come.

Today remember that whatever you commit to the knowing, good, bad or indifferent will ultimately manifest here on Earth.

Thoughts and words and pure intent define the way life flows
When you speak it with intent, it grows and grows and grows.
You propel the energy behind the thoughts you think
Intensity creates the mass like penning it in ink.

Fear creates at light speed, doubt breeds negatives
Any thought that's limited determines how you live.
Speak with good intention, formulate your thoughts
Speak of all your blessings, don't count what you have not.

Change the way you perceive life, those you pass upon the road
Make a choice to see the bigger picture which unfolds.
Heal your heart and take a look at what lurks deep inside
Minimize your ego and eliminate your pride.

For healing light flows through the well where love sweetly abides
Wisdom comes to those at peace from angels and your guides.
You can create at light speed with words and actions too
You owe it to yourself to speak and live inside of truth.

Gratitude

"Celebrating the little things in life will cause the big ones to come."

Let's just celebrate today, the blessings of our lives
Let us count them one by one, for there's more yet to arrive.
Did you know a grateful heart, will quicken blessings so?
Did you know that giving thanks, makes other blessings grow?

Each morning, I awaken, with a prayer of quiet praise
I'm just so grateful to be here, that I count all of my days.
I give thanks for my furry pets who love me lavishly
I'm thankful for the holy well, which fills so many needs.

I am thankful for my friends and all my prayer partners too
I am thankful for my loving home with its warm inviting hue.
I am thankful for the mountains like the ones the greats have climbed
I am thankful for my spiritual gifts and each meditation time.

I am thankful for my body whether thin or voluptuous
I am thankful for the foods of earth all so scrumptious.
I am grateful for the laughter and the great souls on this earth
I am thankful for each one of you, you add to my life's worth.

So count your blessings one by one and feel it to the bone
Praise God in your heart each day, be thankful as you roam.
Remember that a grateful heart will generate much more
Giving thanks each day will open many spiritual doors.

"Whenever you bless anyone or anything, it multiplies the love and encircles back to you".

Bless the water, bless the moon and bless the rising sun,
Bless the life you're living now before the day is done.
Bless those who persecute you and those whom you call friends,
Bless all the animals on earth and to them let's attend.

Bless the rain before the storm for it causes you to think,
Bless the grapes that turn to wine before you take a drink.
Bless the rhythms of the sea as they roll into the breakers,
Bless the souls upon this earth who are God's peacemakers.

Bless the old man on the streets there begging for a meal
Bless the old frau who is sick and pray that she is healed.
Bless the child who has no one to hold and coddle it,
Bless the mother who gave birth with nothing left to give.

Bless the preacher, who espouses truths that aren't your own,
Bless the soul who knows not God and goes through life alone.
Bless the dying and the poor and give them all your light.
Bless the prayers you whisper as you go to bed tonight.

Bless the poet who sends love to you every day,
Bless the souls who hold the faith when you have gone astray.
Bless the earth and all the land that we must appreciate,
Bless the angry souls who try to fill it up with hate.

Bless the prophets be advised that many of them hear,
Bless the God of Abraham who whispers in their ear.
Bless yourself on this grand day for the blessings you've been given
Bless yourself and those you love for the life that you are living.

Today remember that there is nothing quite as sacred as blessing what you eat, where you live and all you hold sacred in your heart.

Karma

It is the wise soul who upon acting asks the question, "Would I want it done to me?"

Often we as humans do things which do not bode
We overlook the consequence to others on the road.
We fail to see that many times we change the microcosm
We fail to see the tiny bee there inside the blossom.

The actions that you take each day affect the world around
Think about the words you say, your actions do expound.
The people in your life take hits through choices that you make,
Many times you do not think and others you forsake.

Would you want it done to you, I pose this simple query,
Would you feel the way they do and wouldn't you grow weary?
Think about the roads you take, the flowers that line the path,
Are there to bring you beauty, not to be the aftermath?

Surrender

"In life there are but two choices acquiesce or transcend"

Acquiesce to the facts of life like bills and death
Acquiesce to good manners and learn some etiquette.
Acquiesce to growing old, your mind and body change
Acquiesce that there are going to be some aches and pains.

But there are moments in each life when you can make a choice
To rise above or walk away or confront with your voice.
There are also moments when the mountain is your friend
It's there to take you higher and to teach you to transcend.

Transcend when things don't go as you had prayed or planned them to
Transcend when rain is falling on the sunny side of you.
Transcend when mountains will not move and find another path
Transcend your ego, recognize that flow won't come through wrath.

Rise above the normal to extraordinary sight
Hold the vision and be praying every day and night.
Live your life as if there were no mountains in your way
The mountains will dissolve when as a tree you bend and sway.

"Personal pain can be transcended when you discover it no longer serves you"

Listen for I tell you that pain is but a choice
You harbor that which serves you and that which gives you voice.
Pain of any caliber stimulates the soul
You seek to find the healing light and that light makes you whole.

Your work may be a catalyst to hang on to that pain
It's where you find a family and blend with those the same.
Many find that they enjoy their suffering way too much
It keeps them feeling something other humans cannot touch.

It often separates you and sifts you from the pack
It often feeds the ego or the strengths which you may lack.
It often is a blanket to keep you warm in winter
Its transforming light can spark you as a teacher or a mentor.

But comes a time to just let go and rise to great new heights
Comes the time to understand that it's only you, you fight.
Comes the time to just forgive and be the grander soul
Comes the season of the wise, pain takes too great a toll.

Today remember to not empower pain by lingering in what you cannot change…for whatsoever you lend your energy to, you multiply.

Humility

*"**Humility** attracts light while arrogance deflects it."*

A humble soul attracts more light than you can here imagine
A humble mind works wonders in a world of disadvantage.
A humble being will produce and yet most will not know
A humble soul speaks not his deeds or any seeds he sows.

Shades of light, cast great streams, on doors closed long ago,
A genesis, to measure faith, and hope within the soul.

I ponder all the miracles many do not see,
I give praise for a heart on fire and what is yet to be.

There are no limits, there are no bounds, if you just surrender,
To all the power that lies within, if each of you remember,
That deep in you there is a well, a river full of blessings,
Anything is possible, when love you are expressing.

Character

"Whatever you hang around with you become."

I know I've taught this lesson but I must reiterate
Whatever you hang out with, will in you create.
Parties through the season will invite you to come in
And act in ways untrue to who you are and who you've been.

Often times we wish to be more liked by everyone
We'll dance upon a table top to be popular or fun.
But inside you'll find the love that you are longing for
Be true to your convictions and you'll draw even more.

So many will encourage you to get off of your mark
To take you down a path on which you planned not to embark.
Many times it's meaningless but for a second there
You want to just engage in fun and let down all your hair.

The price you pay can be quite high since interest will accrue
The price of choosing carelessly is more than most can do.
So take this time to contemplate the choices you have made
Let higher conscious souls prevail on the roads that you have paved.

"To forgive others is divine but to forgive yourself is liberation squared."

Forgiveness is an act of self you give when anger breaks
Forgiveness is what you extend no matter what it takes.
Forgiveness though not easy, is one way to mend a heart
An act of grace you multiply together or apart.

Often we don't recognize that while we've graced another
Our mind is our worst enemy, our own yet to uncover.
Forgive yourself in all you've done no matter what it is
If you don't you'll recognize, what is keeping you from bliss.

Often we forget that we are humans in this race
To make mistakes is just a part of life that we must face.
We have to learn that we are just acting out our roles
To purge or learn or karma heal will benefit our souls.

Forgiveness takes a bigger heart, your pride must melt away
To take responsibility for what you've drawn each day…
Can be the hardest lesson yet, if you'll only see it through
You'll find that in the melting comes a liberated you.

Today may you know the freedom that comes in forgiving others and in forgiving yourself.

Judgment

"Don't judge an angel by the cover...how they look, how they dress and how they act is many times the actual lesson."

His face was young and dirty, his clothes smelled awful foul
His nose was very bloodied but his light shone through somehow.
His actions spoke in whispers, I watched him hold the door...
For a man he knew not when the temperature was four.

I watched him walk so lowly through a parking lot of ice
I watched him thank the people in the cars not once but twice.
He looked so sad and hungry, I couldn't help but feel
And yet there was such magic which would not be concealed.

I had the joy of speaking with this man most would pass by
I had the distinct pleasure to look Joshua in the eyes.
An overwhelming sense of humility burst through
As I write I pray to pass that same feeling to you.

He touched my life in waves and beams I simply can't deny
He caused me to go higher as the tears flowed from my eyes.
Meet me there at Zion and I'll share it with you then
I praise the angels and the Lord for letting me befriend.

You see there's magic in all souls in places you don't look

You see there's God in everything, you've heard don't judge the book...

Give yourself a gift so rare you'll hold it throughout time

Reach out and touch an angel in that stranger passing by.

The greatest measure of a human is the ability to touch another.

Discernment

*"Remember what a person shows you
the first time you meet them."*

The first time that you meet someone tread carefully, assess
How they act and what they say, to you what they confess.
Many times we overlook the things that people say
Many times people reveal inconsistencies at play.

We often will dismiss those things as trivial or trite
What we feel deep in our gut is probably what's right.
We sometimes question ourselves asking if we're being hard
We often doubt our own instincts, our feelings disregard.

In my life experience I've learned my gut is God
I've learned to heed the warnings whether normal or quite odd.
I've learned to watch and listen when another person speaks
So often you will clearly see where truth wanes or leaks.

The smallest indiscretion should tell you to go slow
The smallest acts of deceit reveal all you need to know.
If someone will deceive and lie to the souls they love
What makes you think you're different or that you'll be thought more of?

It isn't that you stand as judge and hang them with aplomb
But what you hang around with you surely will become.
What you lend your heart too will soon become your cage
When you meet this kind of soul it's best to turn the page.

First impressions are rarely inaccurate.

"The Dating Game"

I was feeling oh so vulnerable and yet with brave aplomb
I bowed to an invitation from a man on Match.com.
His smile was captivating, his charm assured me too
I primped in anticipation of this simple rendezvous'.

Married for sixteen years I still had hope, belief
That men were still quite lovely and perhaps would not deceive
I knew myself to be a soul of pure integrity
I thought I'd draw reflections of the good inside of me.

How could I know that in that smile there lurked a darker hue.
How could I know of the date we made, he'd never follow through.
I love people I truly pray that common courtesy
Is exercised in every case with great diplomacy.

Today I wake and understand much to my dumb luck
This man I made a date with turned out to be a schmuck.
No character, no honesty, no balls I clearly think
I thank the universe that from his well I did not drink.

Pathways to Love My Blessing to You

"A single day of selfless giving can wash away a hundred acts of selfishness."

In closing I would like to offer you hope; hope for a better world; hope that one day soon, mankind will see that war accomplishes nothing but death; hope that politicians realize that vitriol accomplishes nothing but dissension; hope that laws change on protecting the environment, animals and human rights all over the globe. My prayer is that all men and women, specifically the gay community, be afforded equal rights and that one day, not too far in the distant future, we will look back and realize that no man has the right to alienate, dictate or deny any other human being that which is innately god given and divine. I would like to offer you hope, that if enough people raise their consciousness, heal their dysfunctional emotions and come together to passionately and productively transform policies and affect change; if millions come together and implement love in all things and let it lead in all ways, that the world will know brighter tomorrows and will thrive for aeons to come, with peace and prosperity flourishing in every nation.

My prayer is that you know what a gift you are to all of life, that you understand your relevance in the world and to life itself and that you step into your roles as gods upon this earth. That you may know and grasp how much can be accomplished through your thoughts, actions and the goodness you pour into the world. My prayer is that you lead with your heart but listen to your soul and use your head in concert with the others, allowing the ego to dissolve. I pray that you envision a world where all men and women, children, animals and the environment, work in harmony in a perfect orchestration of balance, equality for all and deep compassion for each other. Return to love, let it be your soul's greatest remembrance that all things vibrate and are set to the Divine rhythms of love. Love is mastery, become its extension in the world, amplify it and let your lips be found speaking the language of love throughout eternity.

May you as gods upon the earth, walk with the heavenly angels, hand in hand with the Holy Spirit as you navigate all roads and pathways to LOVE.

Acknowledgements

I would like to thank my editor, chief organizer, producer and confidant Robbin Simons for her amazing guidance in the production of this book. You continually amaze me with your wide expanse of business knowledge and the attention you pay to every detail. I am eternally grateful for you and the patience and painstaking time you have taken to help me bring this book to fruition. You have been counselor, consoler, editor, at times mother and a beautiful, creative, spring board to bounce off of. I love you with all my heart and am in awe of your skills and expertise; simply put I don't know what I would have done without you. You are priceless and I thoroughly cherish our connection.

A very special thank you to Dr. Mia Rose, author of "Awaken to Love" and Editor in Chief of "Soulwoman" eMagazine for penning your masterful and more than generous forward for this book. I am humbled to my knees by your amazing friendship, love and support. You continue to inspire me to become even more and I bask in your glow as you blaze trails to help women worldwide become all they were created to be. You are a moving, thinking, breathing work of art and I am in awe of all you have accomplished and what is yet to come. Thank you also for enabling and supporting my "Ask Ariaa" column in "Soulwoman eMagazine" and for continuing to support women worldwide, inspiring us all to be the best we can be. You are a gift to my soul and a treasure to the world. Simply put, I love you.

Thank you to my dear friends William Ball and his beautiful and accomplished wife, Betty Sexton Ball for all you continually add to my life. Your friendship has not only inspired me, but you have become my family and I am grateful to be considered a part of yours. Thank you also Betty, for your wonderful effort and masterful skills as well as the time you took away from your busy schedule to proof read this book. You both add more than you will ever know to my life and I am grateful every single day for the blessing of your friendship.

A special thank you to the beautiful souls I have met in social media since my inception in 2009. Many of you have not only inspired me but you have supported my work, my music and my mission to inspire and uplift millions around the world. I will forever be grateful to those of you who maintained core integrity and who walk the narrow path, the high road every day. I appreciate the years of guttural laughter and joy you have brought into my life and have been profoundly moved and touched my thousands of you. You have made me a better person, I have learned so much from interacting with all of you, from every corner of the globe. Your cultures, your passions and your unique personalities have added richly to my palate. You have my heart, my deepest affection, my gratitude and my undying love.

Grateful for the support of friends, fans and clients!

When you hear Ariaa pray, you know that not only is she directly connected to God but you feel the very presence of God when you are near her. Her energy reaches across miles and everything she has ever prayed for me and others, comes to pass. She is a modern day miracle worker!

~ Joan Wetherford

Ariaa is not only an old soul wise beyond the years of this planet, but also as a great teacher who pays it forward in gracious ways.

~ Derrick Casady

Ariaa is an angel whose words of wisdom travel across continents creating pure joy and unlimited energy.

~ Nadine Haddad

More people like Ariaa would make the world instantly better!

~ Peter Widén

Thank you dear Ariaa for your kind words, I feel honored to know you!! I love your posts ~ your love and zest for Life ~ I admire your ability to write a wonderful & inspiring book, with outstanding sales record~ your wisdom & advice for all of your followers - your ability to chat, listen and give advice on talk back radio shows...you are such a inspiration for women all over the world.... I Love and admire your achievements in Life!! God bless you, my dear friend.

~ Beverley Booth

"Ariaa's presence can be felt from miles away. You'll know her radiance is right in your room, and in your heart."

~ Jefferson Delman

Ariaa brings out in you what you know is dormant under the soul dust that has accumulated over time. Ariaa has helped me pull through one of my most challenging financial times, always stood by me loyally and has given generously of her time to make me see the lessons I needed to learn from it. I'm deeply grateful for her.

~ Lydia Proschinger

Ariaa is a Thaumaturgist!

~*Candy C. Quixly*

Heaven is in her eyes. Ariaa is a visionary, mentor, spiritual warrior of divine light and all who know her are grateful to God for her extraordinary gifts of inspiration for the world and all humanity.

~ *Jane Calpe Valencia*

You are a gift to all of us Ariaa.

~ *Manal Kaakati*

Two roads diverged and I took the one you travel on, and it has changed my life.

~*James Soul*

Ariaa, my sweet funny soul Sista! You bought nothing but light love and positive energy into my life since the day I met you! Wish you as many blessings back as you have given me just by being you! Peace love and happiness my treasured friend!

~*Susan F. Sutton*

Ariaa's pure spirit, spiritual teachings, counseling and love, saved my soul.

~ *Marie Rhoades*

Ariaa is an artist of humanity, who reaches the crevices of my heart.

~ *D. Morse*

My name is Edward and I am a Ariaaholic.

~ *Edward T.*

Ariaa helped me see things from a different perspective. She is mind-changing and mind-blowing!!

~ *Damyanti Robert*

Ariaa shows us the true meaning of humanity.

~ *Joanne Smith*

When I grow up I want to be just like u and have so much love and beauty with in you!! Love you Ariaa. You are a woman who is so selfless and so inspirational and you have touched so many hearts all over the world. You are so loved. A true angel.

~ *Diane Dean*

(Ariaa is) Light and Love personified.

~ *Staci Jordan Shelton*

Ariaa helped me through a time of spiritual darkness. She is a spiritual light in a very dark world. God bless you Ariaa. Someday I expect to see you in heaven and we can talk about all you have given to others.

~ *Craig Hawley*

You make me smile so many times each week and are a light in this world and I love you for that!

~ *Ton Ton K.*

You are amazingly gifted Ariaa, I love to read your postings they are so uplifting and inspirational. Thank you and bless you.

~ *Leigh Gannon*

I agree with Leigh Gannon! Beautiful, inspirational uplifting! You tap into a special world which we tend to forget. Bless you Ariaa, you are a sweet special gift to us all.

~ Cybele Kadagian

She is an amazing breath of life. Over the years, her outreach of love and living life to its fullest has been of great comfort to me and thousands, yes thousands of people. Keep shining Ariaa!

~ Lynette

Ariaa is a miracle! Her healing hands and the wisdom she taught me was invaluable and effective long-term! I don't know how I ever managed without her teachings! And she is FUNNY too!

~Isabella Matz

Great things happen to great people. May your star continue to light the night sky.

~ Michael George Bathurst

You are a gorgeous being of Light, inside and out, Ariaa. I've been repeating so much of what you said to me in my head all day. Bowing in grand gratitude and sending my love to you!

~ Jessica Love Moore

Ariaa, You have helped me in so many, immeasurable ways.... You have a gift so rare, so special and I feel blessed that you have shared and bestowed the sight I needed at a very dark time. I cannot think of the words to thank you, but know in your heart, and mine, that u have placed a beacon of hope, an ability to literally walk again, and the hope of even more triumphant revelations of regaining my strength after my life changing near fatal car accident. You bring me joy, even if we simply leave a brief, but heartfelt moment from time to time. I love you now, and will eternally. You are a lovely, gifted spirit, and I and countless others will forever be grateful. ;*)

~ Linda Wiesen

My life has been enriched in every sense since connecting with Ariaa on Facebook and I have been totally inspired by her warmth and wisdom. I have also been luck enough to talk directly with her which is even more uplifting!

~ Michael Walters

Ariaa accepted my atheism. (She) accepted I was a twisted lost soul who wanted to do David Bowie. (wink)

~ Caroline Cooper

Ariaa is a beautiful woman who touches lives individually - thank you for your inspiration and love.

~Donna Dean Pugh

Ariaa, you are a beautiful soulful lady, with a heart of gold. You are a bright shining light of unconditional love. Thank you for being a wonderful blessing.

~ Lily Wall Flower

Ariaa, I remember when I first saw your blog, I was so inspired by the things that you had written. I was able to relate and that was the turning point for me! Thank You Ariaa! When you accepted my friend request in social media, it was one of my best days of my life! What a gift to cherish, a gift of 'Sisterhood!

~ Josephine Matsutani

"If I hadn't met Ariaa I would be dead by now. Ariaa is a life saver who helped me in my darkest hour to overcome suicidal tendencies and to live a more fulfilling life." ~*Amit Sharma*

Ariaa, I am humbled by your kind words. It is truly my honor to learn and study from you. You have help me transform my mind, perception and reality and it gave birth to real peace and happiness. You have empowered me and helped me find the Divinity within and without. I can never thank you enough for all the good you do for me and all the people you have helped. You are truly an amazing person and I am so fortunate to have you as a friend too! God bless you!

~ Ronald Lew

You are a shining light in a world of darkness.

~ Tisha Elsayed

Ariaa always is blessed by having divine timing in her words ~ deeds ~ actions ~ her songs and music, her Life and Love!!! They all touch her friends and the world and her loving gifts are clearly God given! I am blessed by having a friend and angel like Ariaa!

~ Star Burrows

Thank you for the reminder that laughter is just plain old loving out loud.

~Rick Thorne

I KNEW from the moment we connected Ariaa Jaeger. Thank you. Namaste dear goddess and Soul SiStar!

~Dr. Dheena Sadik

You have a beautiful soul Ariaa. You are very honest and are a beautiful and graceful woman. Your writings provide daily nourishment of one's soul.

~ Sandeep Sanghwal

A woman of great wisdom & a beautiful heart, I simply adore!

~ Stacey Alfonso

You will always be a great inspiration of the heartfelt language ... rock on love.

~ Nancy Morgan

When no one was there to care about me, neither family nor friends, but Ariaa was there. Life was hard. I had a depressed heart and mind and I was done from all corners of life. I did not have a clue what was wrong and why life had been such a mess back then. Ashamed, criticized, and resentful, negativity was taking a toll on me, giving rise to suicidal feelings. I had suicidal feelings to such an extent that I was preparing to die. It was on the night when I was prepared END it all. Being internet savvy, to be more precise, a Facebook addict, I started stalking Ariaa. I wasn't even looking for a solution to all my life problems. I spent hours of stalking and there I was on her Facebook profile, Ariaa Jaeger ('ma'am', I call her now). Just by looking at her picture, I got a feeling that this lady has something for me, that she could help me. I did not know about her, who she is or what she does but I had this overwhelming feeling about her. What made me feel like that?

Without wasting time, I messaged her to see if she could help me. I wasn't even expecting a reply. Seriously, I wasn't! Despite being such a busy personality, it was not more than five minutes I got her reply asking how she could help me. "What's going on, Amit?" Not a minute wasted, I shared everything with her; everything which was troubling me. I shared my every thought with a complete stranger; faith was the only thin thread. Instant replies were exchanged. She told me ways to help myself and gave me sound advice and counseling. Of course, a quick fix was not the solution to problems like these, but she stood by me. She helped me cope through the worst time of my life. She helped me like a friend, and helped and loved me like her son. She gave me mother-like love and care.

Soon, this suicidal and lonesome soul started showing signs of life, learning to shine through all the trouble. I learned to appreciate life, in her very presence. She made me realize why life is a gift, so pure and so worth appreciating, and why life is the ultimate victory to all our sufferings. Blessed I was, and blessed I am; blessed to have such a beautiful friend in my life. Believe me, you won't find a soul so pure, so generous, so kind, or one who loves you as unconditionally as Ariaa does with all her heart and soul. Ariaa is a lady with a HEART OF GOLD.

For me, she was a lifesaving miracle. I am so glad that I survived that night, and that I stood victorious against the dark. I thank you with all my heart and soul, Ariaa Jaeger. I love you with my every ounce of being. Thanks so much, precious. Thanks so much, Goddess!

~ Amit Sharma, India

Ariaa Jaeger
Ariaaisms ~ Spiritual Food for the Soul

Thank you for purchasing "Ariaaisms Spiritual Food for the Soul". I hope you enjoyed reading it and look forward to hearing from you personally. I would deeply appreciate if you would write an honest review of this book, how it impacted you or what you gained from reading it at www.amazon.com.

. *If you would like a special autographed edition of this book, please visit my website at www.ariaa.com*

Wishing all of you blessings on your journey to enlightenment and joy.

Whatever you do, wherever you are and whatever you become, please remember to use your heart and soul to
LOVE OUTLOUD!

With Beams of Love, Light and Laughter,

Ariaa Jaeger

To book Ariaa for personal appearances, television or radio guest appearances, spiritual gatherings, lectures and public speaking venues, voiceovers or vocal performances, you may contact Ariaa directly. To book a personal consultation or session with Ariaa, her current contact information can be found on her website.

Website: Http://Ariaa.com

Facebook:
https://www.facebook.com/AriaaJaeger?ref=tn_tnmn

Facebook page: https://www.facebook.com/BeamsOfLove

Facebook music page:
https://www.facebook.com/AriaaTunes?ref=hl

Twitter: https://twitter.com/AriaaJaeger

Google+:
https://plus.google.com/107140978127037205310/posts

LinkedIn:
http://www.linkedin.com/profile/view?id=25696735&trk=nav_responsive_tab_profilec